ENERGIZE SOLVE PROSPER

Insider Guide To Jumpstart Your Real Estate Investing

Anna Mills

10-10-10
Publishing

ENERGIZE SOLVE PROSPER
Insider Guide to Jumpstart Your Real Estate Investing
www.EnergizeSolveProsper.com

ISBN: 978-1727307894

Limits of Liability and Disclaimer of Warranty
The author and publisher shall not be liable for your misuse of the enclosed material. This book is strictly for informational and educational purposes only.

Warning - Disclaimer
The purpose of this book is to educate and entertain. The author and/or publisher do not guarantee that anyone following these techniques, suggestions, tips, ideas, or strategies will become successful. The author and/or publisher shall have neither liability nor responsibility to anyone with respect to any loss or damage caused, or alleged to be caused, directly or indirectly by the information contained in this book.

Medical Disclaimer
The medical or health information in this book is provided as an information resource only, and is not to be used or relied on for any diagnostic or treatment purposes. This information is not intended to be patient education, does not create any patient-physician relationship, and should not be used as a substitute for professional diagnosis and treatment.

Publisher
10-10-10 Publishing
Markham, ON
Canada

Printed in Canada and the United States of America

Table of Contents

DEDICATION

Dedicated to my mother, Ellen L. Pethe: mother, friend and inspiration to all who met her (1927 - 2017).

I dedicate this book to you. I am the person that I am today because you always taught me how to stay positive, work hard, and be an honest, helpful, and selfless human being. You were such an inspiration on my 1st best seller, and I had hoped to finish this before you left us last Christmas. Still taking college courses at 90 will be an inherited goal also.

She Is Gone

You can shed tears because she is gone. Or you can smile because she lived. You can close your eyes and pray that she will come back; or you can open your eyes and see all that she has left you. Your heart can be empty because you can't see her, or you can be full of the love that you shared. You can turn your back on tomorrow and live yesterday, or you can be happy for tomorrow because of yesterday. You can remember her, and only that she is gone, or you can cherish her memory and let it live on. You can cry and close your mind, be empty and turn your back, or you can do what she would want: smile, open your eyes, love, and go.

- David Harkins

Foreword

Have you ever thought about your life purpose? If you are like most investors, you probably have not. Have you ever thought it was time to transform your life, but didn't know how? Perhaps there are many things you love doing, many things you want to experience and many goals you want to achieve. Perhaps you dream of an extraordinary life.

Again, if you are like many people, your life is filled with activities, obligations and commitments that have nothing to do with your goals or your dreams. You may be spending your life running faster and faster trying to keep up, and at the same time falling further and further away from living that extraordinary life you are dreaming about.

When you transform your life, you will become more interesting, more engaging. You will have a renewed energy, and you will be passionate about your work, and everything else in your life. But to transform your life takes time, passion, courage and a lot of self-awareness.

Energize Solve Prosper: Insider Guide to Jumpstart Your Real Estate Investing is a must-read, whether you are an individual, or one of a group of investors. In it, author Anna Mills shares with you all the great successes and boosts to investing that have come about in her last four decades in the real estate business.

Read this book, and create your own forward *energy, solve* whatever immediate roadblock is in your way, and share the *prosperity* that is there waiting for you!

Raymond Aaron
New York Times Bestselling Author

Acknowledgements

In gratitude and thanks to the Toledo Real Estate Investors Association, and their boards. I am honored to be a leader in Toledo REIA, a nonprofit that inspired me to give back and volunteer. I became an investor within the first year of working as a Realtor. Two rentals, and the house I lived in, was my sole investing for at least a decade. Thinking it was a Realtors meeting, I then accidently walked through the doors of a Toledo real estate investors' meeting.

When it dawned on me that the attendees were investors, I thought I'd died and gone to heaven. Here were dozens of investors that could answer the multitude of questions that drove me crazy for the last ten years. I had never bumped into a single investor in all the years I owned properties—no one to ask questions, no one to help locate parts, no one to bounce ideas off of. The local Toledo REIA even allowed me to become their first female president. Toledo REIA then voted me back again every year for the next 30 years.

From those first real estate investor meetings, I was able to go to the national meetings, and actually meet some of the great teachers around the U.S. I have used all the great basic necessary forms of **Louis Brown,** and the down to earth innovative ideas of **Mike Butler**. They, and others, have kept my feet firmly on the ground, and successful in my business practices.

Thanks to great friends and assistants, like **Dave Czajka**, my right hand vice president; great executive officers, such as multi-functional **Tony Babich;** interesting, energetic couples, like **Mike & Alyce Cervi,** who put in many long hours; and wonderful and knowledgeable board members, **like Judy Pokorny, Joe Burnard, Tammy LeFevre, Dan Duvall, and Lupe Hinojosa,** who have been volunteering by my side every month, for decades, even though they had their own companies to run.

The selflessness and volunteerism of all the REIA associations I have worked with is amazing, and none more so than National REIA. Investors from all over the U.S. donate time and travel, and amazing minds and experience. Thanks to role models, such as their remarkable executive director, **Rebecca McLean**, the dream fulfiller for all investor associations. And I can't leave out the dedication of investors, like Ambassador **Don & Esther Leiby;** and founders, **Tom Hennigan, JC Underwood, Doug Deshields, Scott Whaley,** and **Troy Miller,** just to mention a few of the tireless mentors that were always there for me.

The construction world in the 70s was not exactly accepting of females very often, but **Phil Carter** was trusting or crazy enough to hire me whenever I needed to learn a job. Eventually, Phil even sponsored me for my own contractor licenses, which I needed to work on my own properties. Solely due to his mentoring and patience, I was able to attain more than a dozen multi state licenses and specialty trades to run my own businesses.

Then, believe it or not, and against my own better judgement, I must admit that I have run into quite a few fantastic and selfless government officials. In my political fights for fairness and equality, these government officials were actually working for the people. I only got mired in politics when necessary, so I could be left alone to work my own businesses. Unfortunately, that became harder and harder to do over the years. But I did get great assistance from Mayor **Wade Kapsuekevich**, his assistant, Abbe, and councilmen, like **Sandy Spang, Tom Wisniewski,** and **Rob Ludeman**; and even at the state level, representatives, **Derick Merrin**, and Congressman, **Bob Latta**.

Many behind the scenes experts, like attorney **Jeff Watson**, attorney **Maurice Thompson** of *1851 Constitution,* and **Charles**

Tassel, were always willing to lend their housing and legal expertise. These giants were willing to suffer the media slings and arrows for good causes and affordable houses.

Even before women were popular as realtors, there were people like Century 21 Kasten, **Dwight & Molly Kasten,** and their realtors**, Jan Monica, Yvonne Jacobs, and Sandy Peer**, who were always willing to let me learn from them.

Some younger era ones too, brokers **Jeff Kessler** and **Jason Baker**, stepped up to fill the shoes of Dwight, and take us to the next level, with all the great education. They fulfilled the vision of an educated and trained office, with iLink Realty. They are always willing to assist and take a chance on an investor from way back, even when I did more investing and traveling than office time. Educators, like **Al Meyette & Ivan Smith,** were always pushing me to keep moving forward and learning more. You can't mention great teachers without thanking Professor **Andrew Timothy**, who engineered all the international travels, including my first airplane ride all the way to Australia!

The diversity of all I have learned from my many professions—40+ year realtor, 40+ year investor, 40+ year housing provider, and international teaching—becomes the education I hope to pass on. To continue learning is to continue growing. I learned this from my mother, who still took college classes from Lourdes, into her 90th year.

Sometimes media is your best friend, and often, your worst enemy. You can explain a situation for hours, but the news only wants the 10-second bites that fit their views. Having said that, I must confess that there are a few, like **Fred LeFebre, Scott Sands, Melissa Voetsch, Allie Hausfeld & Tom Troy**, that are professional media, and actually do listen with open minds. When they do try to put a light on both sides, unfortunately, they also get attacked along with the big media professionals, like **Glenn Beck** and **Rush Limbough**. I really like it when they make sure they unite and not divide you.

There are also magnificent organizations out there, ready to assist if you align with them to the benefit of both. **James Caldwell,** of Toledo NW Ohio Foodbank, has been a rich source and an exceptional charity. They are a good match with investors because they could also always spread a donation far and wide to benefit so many with meals. The HBA (Home Builders Association), and PRO (Professional Remodelers Org) are wonderful resources to spread the housing education, and share meaningful and mandatory classes. The Toledo Regional Association of Realtors, and their president, **Jack Amlin,** stepped up many times to help stop the *stupid laws* being passed by local government agencies.

There are also many notable publishers and authors that were willing to assist me along the way. TC Bradley gave me my first chance, and supported me to my first bestseller, seen on www.AnnaMillsPro.

Raymond Aaron, bestselling author of *Chicken Soup, Small Business Branding for Dummies,* and many others, took me under his wing on this venture. I cannot thank him enough for helping on my second book, *Energize Solve Prosper.*

Chapter 1

Paralysis of Analysis

Déjà Vu

Prosperity is about all the hidden sources and resources investors are looking for but do not know if they even exist. It starts with energizing the power of the group, the team. I am not talking about just a partner. Investors are normally loners, out there doing their own thing, getting business taken care of. Investors tend to work on their own, growing their own businesses one day at a time.

Even as they take on help or family to help with the load, it still stays pretty personal. This is about the power of the group to band together to energize each other with a whole third energy—energy that can combine to solve not only the problems of the group but the individual problems of each investor present.

I bought and, for 14 years, rented and managed a couple of houses, not counting the one I lived in. It was a fulltime job that kept me and my 2 teenagers busy constantly. After all, I couldn't afford to pay the mortgages if the tenant disappeared, or if a house stood empty for a mortgage pay period. This went on for many years—close to a decade. Nothing changed and nothing got better, but nothing got worse either.

As time goes by, you learn on the job, and so do the kids. Every little improvement or knowledge helped smooth things out into a tidy little business. Kids grow up, especially teens. You are teaching them how to run a business and make a living, but eventually, they go off on their own.

I used to ask a lot of questions, but most people didn't really understand what I was doing. Half thought I should be rich and lazy, sitting on top of the world, with no work required. The other half that looked a little closer thought it was way too much work. All were outsiders that could seldom answer any nagging questions, except to locate missing parts sometimes.

You really do not bump into other investors, even in a smaller city like Toledo, unless your style was to buy houses at auctions. If you did bump into one, you wouldn't even know it. People kept quiet about it and kept their holding to their selves, and it sure wasn't tattooed on their foreheads. So, I was taken by surprise when my daughter and her neighborhood girlfriend were handing out notices door to door on our street. It turned out that her friend's stepdad was in some sort of real estate field, but not a realtor like me. I looked him up at the Board of Realtors to confirm. So, maybe there was someone right on my own block that was an investor also. Unfortunately, his own daughter didn't really know exactly what he did, but she assured me it was with houses.

Curious, I attended that meeting from the flyer, which I thought was for realtors. I was so sure it was for realtors, I even took my broker and his wife. The city prosecutor was the speaker, and some of the attendees were calling out and shouting that their properties were not being protected. The prosecutor was being very politically correct, but the audience was having none of it. I had been to years of realtor meetings, and there was never a peep from the audience. This audience, with the city prosecutor as speaker, was talking about being *concealed carry,* and taking care of their own properties if the police refused to service their neighborhoods. WOW!

To our surprise, we gradually realized it was a real estate investor meeting, with a couple dozen investors of all kinds. I had not bumped into another investor in all my 14 years. I guess you wouldn't, unless you recognized them as repeat attenders at the local auctions.

I really thought I had died and gone to heaven. Here was a whole room filled with investors, and I could ask all my years of unanswered questions: Where do you find this? How do you fix that? Is this legal? What do you do if..., etc. It was astonishing because I would get more than just an answer. I would get a dozen different diverse answers. The beauty of the multitude of answers was that I could pick the version or style that fit how I ran my rental property business. That's right; the power of the group is all the ingenious ways investors had solved the same problem—all of them great, all of them different, all of them workable. I could even take part of each answer and create my own way to solve each problem.

After about a year at meetings, it had been such a success in my investment portfolio, I decided to volunteer, to be right there in the thick of it—to be able to find answers to my dilemma but to actually hear the answers to questions I had not even thought of yet. The more I gave, tenfold was returned.

One of the biggest concepts that unfolded in front of me with a bang was the *point of critical mass*. I was slowly learning, till it really blew open my mind that the amount of work I was putting into my properties was about the same as those around me that had ten, fifty, or a hundred properties. How did they do this? It was as simple as knowing the concept. The more properties you have, the more funds you have to work with, and the more tenants you can keep in your housing; and the repairs are just duplicates of each other.

Then there was the exact opposite. I did notice that there were several attendees that came every meeting but had not jumped into any form of real estate yet! When I talked with them, they did not feel educated enough, and feared they would mess up till they learned more.

Let me mention a few rules of investing:

1. You never stop learning.
2. You only need to know what you are facing at the time.
3. Everything you learn changes with time.

But the most important of all: The things you worry most about, and look out for, almost never happen. That's right.

When I started, I was worried about three things. Does this real estate investing *thing* really work? Just in case it didn't, I always bought small, single family homes that would resell to anybody in the general public, not just to some smaller pool of investors. I did this for thirty years and, to this day, I have never, ever a sold a single one of my rental properties. Now, don't get me wrong, I have sold properties where I was the lender, and they defaulted back to me. There were no tax consequences. It was the same if I was the contractor and the house came back that I fixed and sold. There were plenty of deductions, such as repairs, mechanics liens, commissions, etc., to keep from creating a taxable event.

What if the houses needed repairs? Again, I always bought smaller homes where I could cope with repairs as a 5-foot female. As far as repairs go, I hired myself out to contractors any time I needed to learn how to fix a repair on my homes. Now I have 14 contractor licenses, 2 real estate offices, and 2 construction offices, and I am president of Toledo Ohio and National Real Estate Investors Association; plus, I manage 65 rentals. So what you look out for takes care of itself, one step at a time.

What if there was a vacancy? I knew that I couldn't pay the mortgages as a single person paid on commissions only. Again, single family homes were what every family wanted, so they had the least vacancy. Plus, I learned really quickly that I could go in at midnight, when the phones quit ringing, and have a whole, 3-bed, 2-story house painted by eight the next morning. That usually made the property fresh enough to show while I was doing the needed repairs.

Forty-two years later, I have never sold any of my 70+ rentals, so real estate investing does really work. Not to mention that most of my thirty year mortgages are now paid off, with several more being paid off each year.

It's ALL in Your Mind

That's right, you can do what you want to do, but you will never accomplish that task if you believe that you cannot.

I had the honor of introducing Tony Robbins once, during an international Century 21 Realtors Convention, in Florida. I learned more from Anthony Robbins in the 10 minutes before we went on stage than I did during the whole conference.

There was a ten-minute delay before we were to go on stage; so, Tony, always a gentleman, offered to teach me to get whatever I wished for in the 10 minutes while we were waiting.

Of course, I immediately agreed—who was I to turn Tony Robbins down? Plus, being only five foot tall, and with Tony's towering 7-foot frame, I felt like I was talking to his belt buckle. So, he asked me to name anything, big or small, that I wanted to do but had not done so far in my life.

I mentioned that I had never been on an airplane, and that seemed pretty darn *cool*. My kids had flown, my grandkids had flown, but I had never tried flying.

He then asked what kind of vehicle I drove. I told him it was a green snoop nose style van, called a Plymouth Transport. Then, the strangest but most revealing question of all: how many identical vans did I see on the road after I bought mine? Of course, my answer was that I saw hundreds of them all over.

Tony then asked if the matching vans had always been there, or did we all buy them on the same day? Again, the answer was obvious that they were always there, but I never paid attention before or was aware of them. Tony laughed and said that was right; the only thing that had changed was that my mind was aware of them, and open to them—nothing more. So, he told me to let my mind do the work for me.

Tony's final instruction was, every time I put my hands on the steering wheel, I needed to repeat that *I was going to fly*. Then Tony made me promise to let him know when I took my first flight. It seemed too easy, and sounded like the fairy tale about Peter Pan and flying.

It was just that easy. All I had to do was open my mind to what I wanted!

Only six weeks later, I was approached by Lourdes College's international business professor, Andrew Timothy, asking me to join him as a speaker at groups in Australia and New Zealand, for several weeks. I was even lucky enough to have my mom, Ellen, join us on these adventures also. From then on, it was nonstop. The next year, we traveled to Cyprus, as our base, and visited Egypt, Israel, Crete, Greece, and six of the Greek Islands.

But the real surprise bombshell was learning that it was all in my mind. I held the controls. What you think and believe is what comes your way, good or bad. What you expect is what you get. That lesson of *saying and believing positive* is what changed my life and every investor I come into contact with. As a five foot female, in a mostly male dominated international world, none believed a woman could do construction or investing.

Thankfully, it is not what the people around you think; it is all about what you are thinking inside, and what you allow yourself to believe. Try it—if a 5-foot, female, senior citizen can do it, so can you.

Don't stop there; it's time to hang around with those investors that are positive, and are positive about you. There's some real insight in *"if you want to be a fireman, hang around the fire station."*

So, if you're an investor, there's a real energy high created when you hang with people who understand who you are and what you do. Not to mention, they are your buyers, sellers, lenders, and workers. They know where to find your missing parts and best workers, or the source to find the perfect partner for the parts you don't like to do: your toughest questions. They don't stifle the entrepreneur in you. You can get a dozen different answers, and use ½ of one, plus part of another, then fit it to how you want to do business.

Belonging to a group of investors can even help put your team together for the things you don't want to do. A *team* is not a permanent partner but someone you use when needed. You might also find a like-minded investor as a business partner, but partners need a lot of due diligence. Some investors might rather have a mentor-student relationship. Other investors might just want to volunteer to get that well rounded view of what other investors are doing in real estate.

FREE is the greatest four letter word in any profession. Putting together FREE 101 classes to bring new investors or visitors up to speed is worth its weight in time. Find a copy of Real Estate 101 Class, in full color, at www.Energize SolveProsper.com.

I always like to share with investors that you no longer need to become a real estate agent, even though I am. Investors should know that most local MLS is FREE to hook into through a local agent. Becoming a real estate agent yourself involves license laws, costly license fees, MLS fees, continuing education fees, and being held to a higher standard if someone is not happy with you.

Worst of all, you are getting a JOB with a broker boss that expects you to perform for his company.

The two options left are finding a new agent to train, or an agent that is already an investor themselves. The reason behind the new agent is simple. With the new agent, you can teach them to perform how you need them. Presenting a lot of low, low-priced offers, run a list of comparable houses sold in the same area as your target house. You can also train them to get you into *good-deal* houses quickly, because time is of the essence when there is a good deal popping up.

The second option is finding an agent that already is an active investor. Finding an investor realtor isn't impossible, but it is a lot easier if you are in a group of investors, because they will be there. Investor realtors are knowledgeable on areas for return on your money, spread needed for flips, and great buy and hold deals. They are also much more up to date on current and new laws that affect your business.

Crazy local and state laws can quickly close you down, or even worse, get you into legal trouble with money, lawsuits, and possibly even jail time. So, pick wisely, and they will be an important part of your team for sure.

I know our city is a little too small for the banks to have their own local REO or foreclosure departments. The only way to get to this style of investments is through a realtor. Quite often, one of the requirements of short sales or distressed properties is having it on the open market for 90 days, with a real estate company tracking the house's showings and offers. This is quite an important asset to investors.

Most of the areas and real estate companies that I work with for my investors, are able to automate the new deals, going directly to the investor as quickly as it goes to the real estate agents. I make sure all my investor clients get a quick showing, the first day on the market whenever possible.

I don't put any personal offers on investor properties till all my clients have decided to pass, or refuse to make an offer. That is never a conflict or problem because, as a contractor, I make offers on the worst properties. The houses no one else wants are the ones I try to purchase and rehab for *buy and hold*.

Millionaire Neighbor

Over the years of investing—42 of them for me—the diversity in the pool of investors has changed dramatically. This is probably true in every other profession too. When I became a realtor, the norm was the male, part-time, *used car salesman* type. You know, the ones in plaid sports coats, that whispered on the phone about *the best deal in town, and hurry, before it's gone.*

I was just a real estate secretary, handling most of the agent's paperwork, clients, and deals, because they were just part timers. I was constantly being teased about getting a license, because I was able to keep everyone current with their buyers, sellers, lenders, and paperwork.

Well, when I saw that there was a test scheduled for the state, I thought I would go ahead and try it. I kept this quiet in case it did not go well for me. After all, there weren't very many female agents around. I did take the test, and I passed the realtor state boards, the first time.

When I got back to the office, I was informed that as an adjoining state, Michigan allowed a one-time testing if you passed your Ohio state boards.

So, I was sent for my Michigan license immediately, because I had passed the Ohio state board with flying colors. Well, my free shot at Michigan, without the taking the courses, went wonderful as well. Well, I passed that the first time—both states— only to get fired as the real estate office secretary when I returned.

You could not be a secretary and hold a license. I guess you might steal someone's clients! What an environment. What a culture shock to go from a weekly pay check to commission only.

Luckily, I ended up in an office that shared tons of knowledge and felt safe enough to never lock their doors or desks. It was definitely a family style office that worked together and stuck together. Forty-two years later, still with the same group but with a lot fewer males, the realtor profession had gone wildly female, and nice and diverse.

I must say, contractors are a little slower to catch up in the diversity realm. In that field, females are still grossly outnumbered, possibly due to the strength needed for much of the work on some of the jobs.

With all this real estate background, I must say it took me only about one year to start adding houses to my real estate life. I accumulated two rentals within the first year, without even trying to go in that direction. It made perfect sense and flowed right into investing from agents.

After all, I was telling all my clients that this would probably be the biggest and most important investment they could make for their family. So why not take my own advice and make investments for myself, a sole parent with 2 teenagers that like to eat—especially when I was going from a paycheck to commissions only. These investments lasted for around a dozen years.

That first investor meeting that I accidently popped into was totally male at the time, and stayed that way for decades. I was actually the first female officer, and the first female president, in our local association. That audience has changed dramatically. As a matter of fact, it actually changed more according to the economy. Changes shifted whenever there were major economic events, especially in the stock market or housing market.

For instance, when Savings and Loans crashed, we had full seats looking for funding. When the stock market got crazy, we got a lot younger crowd that had jumped out of stocks. Then the opposite happened with the housing crash we had in 2005, and again in 2006. Everyone thought the bank repos and the REO were the next big bang.

Truly, I never even noticed such things as male vs female, younger vs older, or ethnicity. I was just focused on getting the job done. Of course, my whole life, I worked in male dominated fields, and just saw them as investors, realtors, and contractors. After all, I had a family to feed, and a decade later, I was the sole support of ravenous teenagers.

As our Real Estate Investors Association grew, and perfected our education and credits, we started seeing a diversity: female spouses, then partners, then owners. The more all-inclusive our education, meetings, classes, and workshops were, the more our attendees exploded in all directions. We have university students, some still taking finals. The boom during the 80s and 90s brought in every neighborhood in the city. Education brought every level and every age group. The stock market crash brought all the suits and techies looking for another avenue for their dollars. Then the real estate crash in '05 and '08 did not lower our numbers but banded us all together to solve each other's problems and panic attacks.

It turns out, it was all about diversity in education, and I will go into some of my great events in the following chapters. For assistance, I have added full-color, full-page calendars of a year full of events, and you can find them on www.Energize SolveProsper.com. Nowadays, I look out into an audience of every age, every size, and every shape.

It's time for another bomb shell. No matter how great the speaker, how interesting the topic, how prominent the education, it is not the most important thing in the room. The important person is not the MC at the front of the room, and it's not the expert that is teaching you. As MC at the front of the room, my job is to get the attending investors to check around themselves. It is the most important thing to get every investor to look around the room.

I am here to tell you that most people do not know who is in the seat right next to them. It doesn't matter how they look— young, old, short, or tall; and it doesn't matter how they dress—suit, jeans, or paint splatters on their clothes.

You can easily be right next to a millionaire or a multi-millionaire. Quite often, they may be the ones in the paint splattered jeans. That's right; everyone–and I mean everyone that you are looking for–is in that very room. There are realtors, wholesalers, flippers, bird dogs, contractors, inspectors, landlords, doctors, lawyers, and judges too! That is just for starts. How about the owners tired of tenants and toilets, the IRA accounts not making any interest on their money, and yes, many million and multi-millionaires.

How do you know one when you see one? How can you tell? Well, it's not by looking at them. It is called networking, shaking hands, giving business cards, getting business cards, and writing their desires on the back. Your whole database is right there in the room waiting for you.

I cannot even count how many times I have been approached to buy our REIA chapter's database–many investors, many more businesses, and even people with a message to get out. But we never sell or give out our members' names and info. To us, it is priceless. Those same priceless names and numbers are gathered in the room with you. The whole pot of gold is right there with the millionaires.

And while you are walking around meeting people, you will find the greatest answers to all your questions, theories, ideas, and comments.

So, who is sitting next to you? Do they have a million in properties? Probably! Do they have millions in 401k, self-directed IRAs, retirement funds? Probably close. Could it be the ones with paint on their clothes, or the ones in suits? Of course. What about the ones that are volunteering and donating their time to assist others? Absolutely. If not, they soon will be, because they are involved, and out there meeting and assisting everyone. Now is the time to meet them. Ask for advice. Get their business cards. Solve some of their problems.

Never go by looks, size, shape, or dress. Meet attendees; meet everyone. Introduce yourself; ask questions. Then, stop and listen. Offer to help; donate time if you think you have nothing else to offer. Keep helping and donating till you find your niche. Keep getting involved until you are the millionaire in the seat next to some new investor.

Where Are the Buyers, Sellers, and Lenders?

If you haven't met that millionaire yet, then you probably haven't put yourself out there enough. You haven't interacted with the person next to you, or the ones around the room. You haven't even asked enough of the investors around you to talk about what *they* do as investors. On the way to getting your neighboring investor to talk, you might find a gold mine bigger than you expected. Most assuredly being in a group of investors makes this networking more fruitful.

Just like any hard to find items, your other investors are the encyclopedia, the yellow book, and the resource, not only for WHAT you're looking for, but for WHO you are looking for. The biggest resource is the investors in the room—not the speakers, not the MC, not the teachers—the investors networking is the largest resource in any gathering.

Just last night, I was talking with a quiet, mild-voiced Bernie, and I learned that he owns airports—that's right, not just houses but airports—and sky diving businesses, and building cars from scratch. You don't learn that from just sitting next to someone and being silent or talking about yourself.

The other businesses investors own are nothing short of varied and amazing. Several people in the room, including a sweet couple, Bob and Helen, and their son, Kevin, were yacht club people, and owned property right on Lake Erie. Dan Rogers, on the board of the yacht club, was very noticeable because he spent the evening making sure all the senior attendees in the room were completely taken care of—such compassion and service to others.

The organizer, Dave Czajka, had volunteered and taken care of all the details of this event for 62 years. If Dave happens to buy in or fund your deal, he will be there every day with his tools, to make sure it gets done. Investors are amazing.

All the board members and volunteers are involved with many, many other associations and projects, boards, and meetings. Yet they still volunteer for FREE, month after year after decades, to bring the new investors their years of knowledge and expertise.

Toledo Real Estate Investors started out with more than 75% as landlords. Of course, we no longer even use the term, *landlord*; only the media and angry government still use that term. We are now referred to as *housing providers.* Coming to the meeting gains you a certificate for the hours invested in the topic taught at each meeting. Adding up the certificates you receive on each topic, can also certify you as a *professional housing provider.* The percentage of landlords in the room has declined but is still over 50% of our local association. Most of that fifty per cent have taken the time and attended the meetings enough to be graduates as *professional housing providers.* So, the other half present in the room are every other type of real estate investing imaginable.

Every single investor (of any kind) really needs to meet and understand how to work with all the other types of investors. We all interact at some point, and more often at several points, during the investment process. It becomes a win-win situation for all involved. Most investors hold many hats, depending where they are in the process of their current deal. They are buyers, sellers, lenders, teachers, flippers, wholesalers, carpenters, electricians, HVAC, and so on.

There are so many helpful events, such as speed networking, mini workshops, Ask the Expert, Buy Sell Trade, Deals and Steals, orientations, and many more.

Another unused avenue is to be the local volunteer. Talk about getting into the middle of the action. Spend just one event checking investor's names at the registration table, or assist at the ever-favorite hospitality table, for a real bonus of name and recognition. Another educational one is to take notes of the questions answered at the *Ask the Experts* table. Sometimes you don't know what to ask, so listening to other investor's questions just opens the mind right up. How about assisting the monthly speaker with his set up, and capturing all those investor *insider gems of wisdom* as you work together for one evening.

If you feel like you don't know anyone, start by handing out name tags or designation tags. You have to inquire of every investor what type of investing they do. That is very good practice to break the ice and ask that question all night long.

As mentioned in earlier chapters, I am constantly asked by investors, vendors, and business partners for a copy of our database. Of course, it is strictly private and off limits. But you are standing and sitting next to the exact same investor contact list you are asking for.

Names and numbers are right there at your fingertips. Shake a hand. Say hello. You can create your own database of essential people that you are looking for. I have even seen business vendors members collect a basket of names at their tables for a drawing, then leave the business cards behind and take the basket.

Everything you are needing, everything you are looking for, is right there in the meeting room. Buyers, sellers, and lenders are all there, and change roles at every meeting. Turn around and say hi! Sometimes you are not even sure what you want or what you are looking for, so start up a conversation. Let the other person talk. You might be amazed at the things you didn't know that you didn't know. Step up when others are conversing. Often, it is truly informative to hear the questions other investors are asking that you didn't even think of.

Remember, too; a buyer this week could be a seller next week, and once he has sold his deal, he could be the lender the following week. So watch out about attaching labels. Labels, jobs, and investments change on a daily basis. Those who already lent the money out, could get a payoff tomorrow if there is a sale. Often, in those situations, it's first-come-first-serve, so get your requests and needs out there. Get your requests and needs out in the public, instead of standing there waiting for the other parts of the puzzle to show up.

After all, they can't let you know their funds are available again unless they already know you are interested. Check constantly. Keep updated on everyone's deals, and what stage they are at, close to completion. Always, *always* ask who they would suggest if they are currently tied up. Lenders know each other, and borrow and lend to each other, and generally know what's going on and what's available and what's not.

Remember, funds are out there, but you aren't going to find them until you are actively looking for them. Keep putting your feelers out. The same goes for buyers, sellers, contractors, etc.

The investors in the room may not even know they are buyers or sellers until they hear from you how good your deal is. Jot the investment down in a flyer or on the back of your card, for quick reference, for those in the room to remember who you are and what you need.

You know the old saying: 90% of the job is just showing up. No matter what, always show up to the meeting. You will always walk away with a gem, a piece of information, or a contact you never expected.

Orientation and Jumpstart

When an investor comes to a meeting, or a group of investors, for the first time, they seem to be overwhelmed with all that's going on, whether it's a large or small get together. It's the first time they've seen a lot of the different people, plus several different speakers or tables at the same time. The first time could be pretty intimidating, with new and unfamiliar terms, deals, and people all around them.

One of the ways to solve this problem is by starting or setting up an *orientation room*. The room has to have some necessities and be staged properly for the best results: chairs, and also tables if possible, and clipboards with applications and pens hooked to them. Be sure to have enough for every single person you have invited to the room. An info folder with all your best information—magazines, newsletters, calendars, and benefits—should be given to every attendee.

Most important is the MC investor at the front of the room. They have to be short and concise, and start mentioning some of the great benefits and discounts, mingled in with audience questions and comments. In the current market, we usually run numbers as high as 20-30 visitors for the orientation room each month.

As soon as I start the regular meeting, and greet everybody, I ask how many new people, new investors, visitors, or non-members there are tonight As they raise their hands, they are invited to stand up and join our vice president at the back of the room, for 10 minutes of special goody bags, prizes, and giveaways, and to get a lot of their basic questions answered. I also mention that they will be back in their seats before the business meeting is over, so they will not miss any of the main topics.

All visitors and nonmembers are invited but must attend an orientation on their free first visit.

I like to proceed with the business part of the meeting so they're never left out of the main topic that they came for that night.

Handling orientation and all the questions and answers is done by one of our board members, plus one or two regular members that have had some recent success to pass on.

All visitors are given a Toledo REIA folder, filled with a lot of our main events and educational offerings. Remember, orientation is set up ahead of time, with tables and chairs, and clipboards with our membership application on it.

The board member at the front of the orientation room starts mentioning half a dozen benefits, and great discounts, local and national, that the Toledo area offers. It's an upbeat basic explanation of what we do as an educational nonprofit investor association.

Visitors are asked questions as to what brought them there, and how we can help them.

The folder with all the information that we are talking about is theirs to keep and take home with them.

Everything is kept moving along, so they don't feel like they're missing anything in the main meeting.

Since they have the clipboard right in their hands, they are offered a 10% discount off of a membership application, if they sign up on the same night. It is also mentioned that our membership includes two members to encourage success.

Besides the membership discount, we also give a bonus Home Depot goody bag, with CDs and discount coupons, if they sign up the same night.

They can sign up right on the spot and get all their goody bags, or they can sign up any time before the end of the meeting. When they sign up, they are also given a Toledo REIA binder, filled with all of our basic information. It contains our disclaimers, bylaws, and state landlord, and tenant laws, etc. That notebook is also used to collect all the free forms and information that are given out at every single meeting for those in attendance.

Our immediate sign-up rate is close to 50%. The new members are introduced to the Home Depot discount tables, and to all our great vendors in attendance.

Orientation is a very important introduction to real estate investing and Toledo REIA, as a step to help visiting investors understand what is going on. It puts them in a safe place that encourages questions. It also gives tons of information, if they don't know what questions to ask. Just listening to others ask questions helps a lot as well.

When they come out to join the local investor members, they have a better idea of the basics, and can relax and join in the following education, knowing how it changes every month.

Another handy program that I initiated (get a full-page

checklist, at www.EnergizedSolveProsper.com) for our new members is called Jumpstart. Just like some members are more interested in the education designations, some are more interested in moving quickly. They have already decided on real estate investing and want to integrate and move along fast.

The Jumpstart program looks like a bingo or checklist of a dozen different actions that the new investor member can do. The purpose is to familiarize the new investor member with all the different items going on during our jam-packed monthly meeting.

The Jumpstart program can be done as quickly as the member wishes. Most of the checklist refers to things that can be done within our meetings. It pushes new members to meet and greet several vendor members around the room, and get acquainted with their great services and benefits.

It also pushes new members to meet or even assist several board members at the meetings while they are getting the meeting set up. Then, of course, we have several events that the new member needs to know about and try out, or even attend on a regular basis.

There are different things happening all around the meeting room, so these are listed for the new member to check off as they search them out. It makes them very familiar with all that's going on for the investors.

It orients the new member with our Wednesday, *One-on-One*, at the local salad bar. They can ask any questions about real estate investing or Toledo REIA. It also calls for a visit to our Friday breakfast meeting, in the private room at Uncle Johns Pancake House, with several of our vendor members.

It also makes them aware of the great Saturday workshops we have for all members that want to delve deeper and be trained on our Tuesday topic.

Many of the things mentioned in this guide don't fit each and every investor. It is designed to assist all styles of investors and entrepreneurs.

Chapter 2

Captivate the Investors - Kindergarten Rule

Be Affirmative

I've talked about being positive at the very beginning, and I cannot emphasize how important that is to the whole atmosphere when you're together with a group of investors—no moaning and groaning about the government or the economy. Instead, if you are happy, and if you dwell on the good and positive things, real estate is good. If you're excited, then real estate is exciting. As a matter of fact, the very first thing on our agenda at every board meeting is that *we're only looking for happy, positive, affirmative investors.*

It's about being positive, because we set the atmosphere of the room, and that is exactly how that get together will run. And it is exactly the feeling that everybody, and the investors, will walk away with when we're done. So, if you're having a bad day, come to our meeting to get the positive side. If you can't shake the negativity, don't show up at our board meetings. It is the board that I expect to set the tenor of the meeting. If the board cannot do it, how do they expect the meetings to run upbeat, and have the investors want to return?

Our meetings are exactly the place the upset investor can set things right. That's also an underlying rule for keeping people interested in the audience. If you are down and complaining, don't expect success. Investors are a single business structure, most often in a world that does NOT understand real estate investing. A meeting of their own kind is the only place they can relax. They can enjoy themselves and have fun. They can get the missing part or the missing answers to the questions, where no one else even understands the question.

I had several dozen houses, and my father still asked when I was going to get a real job. But he did call on me when he wanted his roof redone, or to learn how to side his house.

If you keep saying that you don't see it, you won't. If you keep repeating that you can't get ahead, you won't, because you are talking to your mind and shutting it down.

To keep up the energy and the attention of those you are talking to, make it fun and interesting. If you are boring, or if you are trying to explain your point six different ways till every single person in the room gets it, you will have most of the room snoring. Instead, move along, and people will ask if they need more information.

It's not rocket science, but lots of investors show up after work, or after a full day of investing, and you have to keep them awake if you want to get the rest of your message across. It has to be educational, informative, and FUN!

It is also a very positive feeling for them to get the free forms to add to their Toledo REIA association binder. They may not need this particular info right this minute, but it will be in their binder when they do need it.

Also, just before introducing the speaker, we take a three to five minute break to move around and visit the vendors around the room. Let them hear good benefits and discounts from every business partner who took the time to be in the room.

The simple rule is to be positive, and keep them engaged and having fun, so they will hear your message.

Being positive is a fulltime job; everyone wants to tell what went wrong that day, that week, or that month. But investor meetings and get-togethers are not the places for solutions to those disasters or problems. Start asking who had a buy. Who had a sale? Who had a deal? Who had a steal? Throw out a bonus to those that get things started.

I know, as a housing provider, we all tell our horror stories, and not a single person talks about the 50 checks that arrive at one time each month. After all, war stories are much more dramatic to tell. But think about that new member listening, and the picture you are painting about your business. Save these stories, good or bad, for the Christmas party game, The Good, the Bad, and the Ugly.

Another positive practice would be to give members a 10% discount for every guest they bring that signs up. That's pretty positive. And announce it in front of the whole group.

Even when we make announcements about the government, called The Good, the Bad, and the Ugly, it makes me search for at least one thing good about them.

Also, keeping things positive, we declare that once something is voted on, there is no longer any negative discussion. We will all come together for the results of the vote, as a team should; there is no negativity if the vote did not go your way.

Be Active

As with any good group of investors, it is best to keep them actively engaged. Once I start a meeting and start giving out information, I like to poll our investors, keeping them invested in what we're talking about. Everyone takes a seat after the pledge of allegiance, but not for long. After I introduce myself, I ask how many members are in the room. I follow up with asking how many nonmembers, visitors, or 1st time visitors are there. They are asked to stand and visit our vice president, Dave, for orientation, and for goodies and gifts, and then to return shortly.

Then we start asking for different styles of investing, and to raise your hands so the audience can see what investors are present. I ask them to raise their hands if they are a buyer, a lender, a seller, a lead contractor, etc.

We also ask all Toledo REIA members to keep hands up till they receive this month's special FREE handout.

Before that commotion dies down, we start asking for volunteers to hand out our FREE new app for the month. As that is going on, we start our *Good Better Best* new benefit for the month, and ask for volunteers to pass that to members with their hands up.

We then talk about *the good, the bad, and the ugly* government, to get everyone stirred up and asking questions. After that activity, we have them sit down, and we teach them about government red flags.

Next, on the agenda, is the *Buy, Sell, and Trade*, involving the audience to call out any available properties, etc. We encourage them to line up to the microphone and give their announcements. The bonus for standing and announcing it themselves is that they get a free printed ad in the newsletter, the **Investor Survival Journal.**

Then they sit while we explain the PHP (Professional Housing Provider Program). They are told what topic they will receive a certificate for that night, and where to pick it up at the end of the education session.

Also active would be any benefit, discounts, or specials from our business partners. You must visit the business partners table to be in any of their drawings. Then flyers are passed around so they have the necessary info when needed. After that flourish, it's time to sit down again while we list the upcoming calendar for the rest of the week and month.

To get investors back in their seats, we call the vendors up with drawings. You have to be in your seat to win. With excitement and enthusiasm, I introduce the speaker or topic for the month, and get them all excited to learn. Truly, they are probably just excited that I will now go away and leave them alone for a few minutes while they learn from the night's speaker.

This technique is probably more commonly known as kindergarten style.

It is simple: you need to give the ones you are addressing something active to do; then let them sit down; then actively pass something out; sit down; take a survey by a show of hands; sit down; ask for audience participation in buy, sell, and trade; then sit down.

By the time I am done, within our short (thirty minute) business meeting, investors are more than happy to be left alone to quietly listen to the main teacher.

Before I get to the speaker on stage, there is a very active break where we let the investors grab a bite to eat, visit the vendors, or network.

To get them back in their seats on time, we announce that you have to be in your seats to win. We go from that quiet sit-down to being active throughout the night, till the intro to the night's speaker or topic. I try to cover something for everyone but keep it interesting to every investor in the room.

It sounds simple, but you must crowd several hours and tons of information into approximately thirty minutes, to get it out to all investors.

You drive the positive meeting, or the conversation, with your positive attitude and excitement.

Plenty of Goodies

I mentioned all the flyers, forms, and information I share whenever there is a gathering of investors— starting right at the front door, at visitor check-in. New investors are given a disclaimer to sign for the content, their own due diligence, and the possibility of tapes and video. Our meetings are streamed to many other states, like California, Tennessee, LA, Texas, New York, and Perrysburg.

Name tags are put on to help identify you. We also have investor tags if you want everyone to know what genre you are working on currently. Visitors receive a map of the meeting, and an invitation to the orientation room, along with the discount coupon for signing up that same night.

Current member investors are given name tags and a sign-in page to make sure their contact information is correct. Also, everyone who enters can attach, to their name badge, ribbons that identify their specialty: wholesaler, housing provider, flipper, buyer, seller, lender, or business partner.

There are more gifts and info all around the room at the vendors' tables, with all their discounts and prizes. There's also an advanced *Ask the Experts* table, where all real estate and Toledo REIA questions get answered.

Within 5 minutes of starting the meeting, all nonmembers are invited to go to a 10-minute orientation. At this meeting, their questions are answered in the overview of Toledo REIA. They are also given a real estate magazine, event calendars, and discounts, for an overview, in general, about real estate investing. New investors are also given a 10% discount to sign up that night.

The member investors in the general meeting are receiving flyers and magazines on their chairs. All members receive their free form and free app for the month. There are also info sheets handed out during the *Good Better Best,* on new benefits and discounts, and handouts for everything that's going on in the government, the community, and the local investor world around us.

All members have the Toledo FREIA binder, with all the basics in it about real estate investing. These include forms, laws, and information handed out to all investors attending the meeting. All this can be stored in their binders if not needed right away.

Members also get the wonderful bonuses, like five different discounts at Home Depot improvement stores, and 60%-plus off goods and printing of office materials. Investor members are also given discounts by every single one of our 50-plus vendor member business partners.

Each and every one of our vendors gives a discount larger

than the cost for membership as an investor. It usually takes only one visit to any one of our business partners to earn back the price of membership.

Investor members network and get tons of free advice from the other local investors that have *been there and done that.* A mistake by any one investor can now be shared with all investors to keep them from the pitfalls. Investor members willingly let you know where to find some of the hardest things to locate for running your business. An investor member will freely educate you on what tenants not to rent to, what businesses not to go to, and what government rules not to ignore.

Any of the investor business partners that we have, not only give you great discounts, and great information, but they also bring one or more prizes to give you at every one of the meeting sessions.

All investors love the four-letter word beginning with 'F'... FREE. Investors are always looking for the deal, and where there is a pool of investors, they freely offer deals back and forth to each other, and to you. It is not uncommon for a realtor investor member to give free MLS access to the other investor members.

Our attorney investor members even donate free answers to your legal questions at the meeting, without sending you a bill, as long as you're respectful of their time.

Good Better Best

One of the toughest jobs to distribute and keep at the forefront for all investors is the long list of benefits that have been accumulated over the years.

Benefits are numerous, important, and ever changing. Benefits are a unique marketing tool, because investors are only interested in them when the time comes that they personally need them. When you need that particular service or answer, then it is all important.

That is why I prefer to give them out in flyer or coupon form, so investors can find them when needed. Investors really need a tool belt to hold all the great benefits. That is one of the reasons we provide a Toledo REIA organization binder, so they can find them when they desperately need a particular one.

Good-Better-Best is another way to spread out all the great benefits and discounts that can be used when we all work together. Good-Better-Best is a chance to get at least a full description of three top benefits each month. It is hard to give a full roll out list of all the great benefits available. This announcement is used to make sure new visitors and current members know what discounts are also all around the room at the vendor tables.

The list of benefits and discounts is actually so immense that it is hard to keep on top of it. Quite often, an investor asks about a certain discount when they are in the middle of the problem already. That investor only needs a particular discount when that situation pops up. So, it's a fulltime job to keep investors aware of all the different specials that they can use and have access to.

Every business partner, who is a member, wants to make sure that their products and services are in front of all the investors. Business partners want investors to be aware of them when they are looking for that particular product or service. The more the investor uses a number of business partners, the more we can add with a better discount. And the more that the business partner is used, the better deal they do for the investor. It's a circle that needs to be completed for both sides to be satisfied.

One of the reasons that I have orientation at every meeting is to get across a smattering of our discounts and benefits to new people in the room. But almost as important as money, is the time and aggravation our members save by using all the great discounts.

We are constantly bringing in discounts, bonuses, and prizes from all 50-plus of our local business partners. There are also tons and tons of discounts from national real estate investors, plus we also have a few things going on at state level.

None of this works unless we make sure the investors know each benefit exists. Even the home improvement stores have a table at every one of our meetings, just to make sure you are signed up for Home Depot's five discounts, and you have corrected your credit card numbers as they expire or change.

Having the business partners attend, in person, helps explain to the members and investors how great their products and services are, and how they work.

Good-Better-Best also works if you can make some gains into reminding the attending investors of the discounts. It really needs to be a positive sounding announcement that gets everyone to start taking notes. Normally, government issues have to be put under *the good, the bad, and the ugly.*

This special announcement also goes well with the flyers and handouts that you can give to local investors. It is another great way to keep a meeting positive. There's nothing more positive than giving out bonuses and discounts to save investor's money and time.

It is the session we give away and hand out most to the attendees. It even becomes a reason for some investors to attend and not miss any meetings.

Buy Sell Trade

Buy, Sell, and Trade is definitely an audience participation event. It goes by other names also, such as *deals and steals*, but generally follows the same context. It is a venue that allows the attending investors in the room to do business with everyone else in the room. It's a forum for an investor to throw a deal or a request to everyone in the attendance.

Buy, Sell, and Trade can run for a whole meeting, or just be a designated part of it. I like to use a clipboard for investors to pre-sign up as soon as they enter the room, so we have a general idea of how much time is needed.

If we are short on sign-ups on the clipboard, I will ask the friendliest, most bubbly person in the room to take the clipboard, row to row, for volunteers.

Variety is good. I've had an investor sell a whole house for one dollar at the meeting. Of course, the challenge was that it had to be moved off current land it was sitting on to someplace else. It was bought immediately by a truck driver that moved houses for a living. What a success story.

Sales can be everything and anything to do with real estate or investors. You will also be really surprised at some of the businesses that other investors run. It's a real eye opener.

For some control and uniformity, it helps to keep the session moving right along. Although one investor can explain a great deal to the attendees in one sentence, the others aren't finished in more than half an hour. I prefer to have instructions right up front on the Buy Sell Trade clipboard sign-in sheet, allowing a thirty-second presentation for each person signed up.

If time is scarce, it also helps to be in control of the microphone. If the MC is holding the microphone, and things are running too long, it's easy just to announce, "Don't forget your phone number."

On the other hand, if you're not getting enough people to sign up, throw in a bonus. The bonus that I use is a free one-line ad in our newsletter, the *Investors Survival Journal,* which goes out to thousands of investors.

Another good way to get shy investors to start signing up is to already have a few deals listed on the clipboard. Another way to drum up ads is to have an assistant take the clipboard around the room for one last sign up.

In most cases, the clipboard gets too full to fit in our tight time span. To help, I leave instructions to bring the clipboard up to the front of the room as soon as there is ½ dozen investors signed up—or whatever number is needed to fill the time slot you have set for *Buy, Sell, and Trade.*

There's no one better at explaining a deal than the investor that is working on it. That is why, even though they're already on the clipboard, I really prefer to have the investor, that knows the deal, make the announcement.

If there's a question that gets yelled out, they are present to answer it. Plus, they are personally giving out their phone number, for any questions to be sent directly to the investor. Plus, who is going to be more passionate than the investor working on the deal or needing assistance.

This has been a very popular benefit to buyers, sellers, and lenders. It is an important event because it gets the investor up and moving, and they are reacting with the investors in the room.

It is also helpful because, then, investors start recognizing each other. It helps to create ties with all the investors. It brings them together, because most of them are buyers, sellers, or lenders themselves.

Active Hidden Calendar

The calendar of events is a necessary evil. Investors need to plan ahead for your events. I worry that it allows some investors to pick and choose, rather than attend all meetings on a regular basis. Of course, I prefer they attend all meetings, with all the great information given each month. So, I like to use it sparingly. What I mean is, we obviously have to use a calendar, and it is put in all our publications so that the investors and the public know all the great education that is available. Again, I use it in small doses.

If we do use it in our newsletter, on our website, and at our meetings, I try to not publish any more than 2 to 3 months ahead. Instead, 90% of our literature is signs on the street, and our advertising boldly mentions that our meetings are always the second Tuesday, every month.

For one thing, that is actually easier to remember than any particular topic or date.

The reason for not publishing the whole calendar year of events is so that your investors don't decide to just pick out their favorites. I want every meeting to be important. I want all investors, at every meeting, to learn, get updates, and stay knowledgeable about what's going on in our local area.

Near the end of every meeting, before people leave, is the perfect time to get all excited about the next meeting coming up the following month. Again, I want to excite over one hundred investor members, to attend every one of our monthly investor meetings.

While the calendar is in hiding, with only one or two months being published at a time, there is a flexibility with changed topics. That way, the focus is on what is going on right now at this month's meetings.

On any given month, we run at least five meetings, including a board meeting and workshop, minimum. That is more than enough for investors to concentrate on at one time.

The calendar is always populated with the reoccurring events, such as trade fairs, shark tanks, and end of the year holiday parties. Then there are programming contracts, with approximately four big name speakers yearly.

The calendar's filled up with the great topics from the PHP (Professional Housing Provider) manual. Even though the calendar gets finished, it is still not shared till a month or two ahead of time.

On the calendar, I also include important state and national REIA events upcoming. So travel events are posted as much in advance as possible. Also posted early are workshops and anything that needs reservations. On the calendar, we also have any event that may close out quickly, leaving investors out in the cold because they are all filled up.

In between each monthly posting, the calendar reminds

everyone to go to the website for more detailed information. Because of the weather in our area, we also post that our meeting will be closed whenever they close the roads. I'm pretty sure that happened only once in thirty years.

I like to include the full past calendars in the visitor's packets. This gives someone new a more complete look at all the speakers, topics, and meetings we provide. The calendar is also used in advertising and marketing for more great business partners.

There are many places the Toledo REIA calendar can always be found. It is always published on the first inside page of the newsletter, *Investors Survival Journal.* It is always tabbed on the front page of our website, wwwToledoREIA.com. It is posted on all our social media pages. It is e-blasted to our member database. It is also sent to city council and the mayor.

Calendars are one of the best forms to hand out at the orientation meetings.

Chapter 3

Good Bad Ugly

National REIA

Being at Chapter level of National REIA has more benefits than I can even mention. One of the best is the connection with all the other investors around the nation. If they fall in a pitfall, and share it, then I don't end up in the same hole. The worst offenders are usually the federal, state, and local governments. They are always coming up with strange ideas and even crazier laws that they think will fix the world. Of course, the funding for all these wild projects comes from the investors pockets. We are known as deep pockets, with all those rents we collect. Whatever dangerous idea pops up in one community, will spread like wildfire to everyone's home town. Somehow, it looks like free income to them.

One of the ways to check out what's going on around the country is called the *Good Bad Ugly* session. My original lesson was *Good Bad Ugly* as an event at the National REIA level that tracks all good and bad that happens all over the U.S., for all the local chapters.

This session is held nationally every year, for investors from all over the United States. It covers everything and anything to warn investors about bad and good speakers, courses, teachers, books, government, rules, laws etc. If one group of investors in a particular area has troubles, it is passed on to all other investors around the United States.

They go into detail, so everyone knows what the problem is, the size of the investor group, and the size of their area. After the facts are gathered, then they are asked what they have done so far. What has worked, and not worked, is important.

This gives such a heads up to our local investors, to know what to look for in our papers, media, and councilmen. Unfortunately, all government departments have their own seminars to find more ways that other areas have charged fees, charges, and penalties.

Good Bad Ugly became a yearly event by popular demand of the local investors participating. National REIA's version is done behind closed doors, and minutes are not taken. A lot of the educators are rated and, therefore, excluded from the room so that everyone feels free to tell it like it is.

Information like this is jotted down for what pertains to your local area. At least there is a heads up for any trouble that looks like it is coming towards your area in the near future.

It is also eye opening to see what some of the tribulations are for different size groups of investors, or different parts of the country. It is also amazing to see that the million dollar (mansion) property is the same size as one of your rental properties, at twenty thousand dollars. Location, location, location—right?

Let's not forget that there is a *Good* in *Good Bad Ugly*. The litany of good things that are happening around the US seems to get longer and longer each year. Bravo! Also, those are the things that we want to replicate in our own area for all of our investors.

Good Bad Ugly teaches our local investors who to have for a speaker, and who not to have for a speaker—or at least what to look out for with particular speakers or vendor products. Also, learn what to add to our contract for each particular speaker.

Not everything that comes up is the speaker's fault; maybe it's not even the investor's fault. Quite often, it is just a learning experience for everyone to take advantage of so it does not happen locally.

State

Closer to home is the state level. Hopefully, your state even has an association to help local investors along. There are only a few state organizations at this time. I know that National REIA has assisted in trying to start a half dozen of them around the US, in various states. Some of them are still just fledglings, and some haven't quite got it together yet.

Most state groups are used for legislative issues at the state level. Pennsylvania has a huge government presence, called PROA. Of course, they offer huge discounts on all your utilities too.

Ohio is lucky enough to have a state association for more than thirty-plus years. Ohio is legislative also, with a political PAC group but also spread into speakers and discounts. I know they have only a few vendor members, but they do have a large conference yearly. Investors can go check out speakers selling their courses, and some vendors.

I attend to see which speakers have something educational that fits into my local area.

Ohio fought a very large case recently on Fair Housing. The actual story is pretty long. Basically, an eighty-year-old housing provider was targeted by *fair housing testers*, 8 times in a row. So, it is important to be educated about pets and comfort animals. You also cannot be too helpful, and can mention units that might work better for a tenant than the one they are looking at.

The way the media reported seemed like the normal question and answer anyone would give without even thinking about it. The question she asked was regarding a prospective disabled tenant with an animal: "Who would be cleaning up the backyard?"

That was enough of an answer to have Fair Housing send secret testers back, time after time. One time, an interested mother, with many children, took a look at her duplex. Her duplex had carpet in the lower unit and hard flooring in the upper. She suggested it might be more sensible to rent the lower unit for noise control, and she was trapped again.

I'm not sure about her area of the state, but I have been told that our local Fair Housing gets their salaries paid by the money they raise, by lawsuits and penalties.

Entrapment is legal, it seems, along with being personally sued by the tester as well. Even though they were not really looking to rent or buy your place at all, they can sue for damages. Remember, civil rights is the only case where you are presumed guilty, and must prove your innocence. Normally, they expect you to pay their fine and walk away. With up to a one hundred thousand dollar penalty, she refused to give in.

Therefore, rules and laws were changed by her toughness. She could not have done it without the assistance, legally and financially, from both 1851 Constitution, Ohio, and National REIA.

Great lawyers jumped in, like attorney Jeff Watson, and attorney Maurice Thomson. You cannot thank these brave people and organizations enough that jump in when they are told lawsuits are unwinnable.

Benefits like these are then shared by all. It's another great reason to stay in touch and share what everyone else knows about what's going on in the rest of the state.

Don't forget or underestimate the power and creativity of networking with all the investors in different areas. It's the entrepreneur in them that has changed their business, with a great twist that will blow your mind.

And that will be one of the first ones on *Good Bad Ugly,* the following year.

Local

We, as investors, can partner up with the local realtors' board, the local builders' association, the local remodelers' group, and many others. These groups may all be real estate but not always on the same side of the vote and any particular issue. Most often, we are on opposite sides, vying for the same market, or same real estate deals, but for different reasons.

As local investors, we get most of this information from National Real Estate Investors, but our local *Good Bad Ugly* is usually about the government or the utilities. Locally, we use the Good Bad Ugly session to warn of all the political potholes in the roads for investors. It helps them steer clear before it is too late.

In my local area, I have sat on many different committees in self-defense. I have been on the Lead Paint Hazard committee for close to 8-10 years, and many other different administrations. They have taken the same piece of legislation through a half dozen name changes and many transformations.

It was dragged through as Point of Sale, but homeowners screamed. Next was Point for Rental, for the same fees and charges, but the big apartment complex owners screamed even louder. This last time, it was referred to as *Save the Children,* and was all about Lead Paint Dust Free inspection fees.

I was sitting on this committee for a decade. I realized, when we started all over at every meeting like it was our first, government was a whole different world. To them, it was a day to get off work early. Nothing had to be accomplished, and getting things done didn't seem the matter at all. I, on the other hand, was losing time, work, and energy, just to stop a law with no common sense.

Other committees that you need to keep a pulse on are water utilities, who are raising the water/sewer/ trash fees three times a year. Another is Safe & Healthy homes for green appliances. The health care field is actually demanding pages of questions answered before you can get any health care aid— questions like rating their plumbing, heating, airtight home, energy appliances, pests, etc.

City council committee meetings pop up tons of land minds, and show what crazy new taxes they are thinking up; and city council board meetings are the only ones you can sign up to speak, just to name a couple.

It's astonishing to say that I have been in as many as 23 meetings within a one-month period. It is exhausting and mentally frustrating because of the lack of anything ever being finished.

It depends on what type of hot new rules and laws are being passed yet again. Lawmakers never seem to learn that it is almost impossible to make a law encompassing a whole profession, especially a profession that they do not understand themselves. They usually have never run such a business, or know all the ins and outs.

There are unintended consequences when they try to blanket everyone with one law. One size does not fit all. They fail to see that the unintended consequences are often worse than the situation they were trying to correct to start with.

We are still suffering locally, due to the *Predatory Lending Law*. Lawmakers on the east and west coast never took into consideration that their law, by nature, cuts out all loans under fifty thousand, and sometimes under as much as seventy-five thousand.

They all didn't know, or forgot, that the whole mid-west has houses in the fifty to seventy-thousand dollar price range, all day long. As a matter of fact, my city has almost one hundred houses under ten thousand dollars, on the market currently, listed with realtors.

What you don't know...can put you out of business!

Solutions

I'll cover banding together and chipping away techniques on upcoming laws in the next chapters. Let's get into some online solutions. They actually cost very little, or are free. Luckily, National REIA willingly carries the master plan, making it affordable, and sometimes even picks up the fees.

Voter Voice is a system that gets you through all the red tape, straight to your very own state and national government officials. With government officials afraid to open their mail, you never know what form of media they will open or actually see.

It's a grassroots advocacy platform that creates modern campaigns to tell your representative what your views are and what you want or need. It can mobilize investors and supporters to reach out to lawmakers, with a touch of a button.

It can even promote on social media, whether you are tech smart or not. You really get results through these responsive emails. I can easily post comments on regulatory forms and through multiple channels. The days of envelopes and stamps has evolved.

It is such a great tool for investors who are not hooked into big bucks lobbying systems.

It automatically gets through to your particular state representative, using just your zip code. It also supplies the form letters needed, with all the necessary headings. This is a form letter where you can make any personal changes you want, and send it directly to your particular government official.

Another wonderful tool that we can offer is *Bill Tracker*. It's an online system that lets you know exactly what the lawmakers are doing with any bill or law in current time. Every time a bill goes up through the next hoop or committee, it immediately gives you the results.

It impacts more policy with all the lawmaker analytics for those that want to delve in deeper. There's legislative tracking right down to email alerts for the laws you're most interested in.

This is true monitoring in real-time analytics across all fifty states, and all kinds of legislative social media and comparison tools.

Actually, Good Bad Ugly does force me to search out and find something *good* in the government as well. It also forces us to meet, greet, and get to know the beliefs of the local city councilmen. It teaches us to form alliances with the like-minded players whenever possible. It helps give the ones on our side of the issue, the support and backbone they need to not be bullied into a vote.

The greatest benefit by far is the ability to alert and inform investors what is going on when there is an emergency. It brings everyone onto the same page, instead of listening to rumors and stories. It can be a call to meet at city council, or to call your local representatives, or a warning of what happens when you vote wrong.

I am sure there are many more great programs out there also. I really look forward to their discovery by National REIA, or by one of my local investors.

I have a great board member, Tony, who brings to all the hundred-plus investors in the meeting, a new FREE app for their phone every month—month in and month out, for years. This is such a commitment to assist all his fellow investors to the next level.

Banding Together

Is there protection in numbers? Yes, I think so. Be sure to thoroughly check who's in your local band of members, and exactly what their view is on each issue as it pops up. In a lot of the cases, you have to offer your take on the issue, and try to explain what their side might be. Always follow up with the unintended consequences that would sneak up on them if they don't ally with us.

Banding together with all these real estate groups is not usually as helpful a defense as you might think.

They may be against the new bill or law, but willing to throw us under the bus. In the very least, they shy away from supporting us on issues, because they are big enough to get themselves removed from the crazy laws. So, they probably would vote against us just to get the law finished, while they are excluded.

Every time an investor gets stung or blindsided, he shares it with all the local investors at the meeting. I am always open for these upcoming catastrophes, and want them highlighted in front of our whole membership.

By announcing these pitfalls, other investors can input how they may have gotten around, or successfully fought, that very same problem. Sometimes I am lucky enough that some other investors have already created some case law. I always present this info with great etiquette and respect, and not throw it in the face of the judge. The insights from like-minded investors, battling the same problem, really helps each other. I must say that the solutions they come up with are often just pure genius.

The *Good Bad Ugly* gives investors a chance to protect themselves from the danger of all the rules they don't even know exist. We send a lot of alerts out to investors after we attend a national *Good Bad and Ugly* session, to spread the information.

These alerts, hopefully, get the message out and help to track different bad laws and their continual changes. I know that the *lead abatement rentals law* in our area has had twenty-three changes, even before it had gone into active status. It also gives investors the opportunity to join these government committees, and to get things inserted or corrected in the bad laws.

Even small changes can actually put an end to the offensive law, or change it to become a moot point law.

I really like the *Vacant House Law,* from several years ago, which was going to rid Toledo of all the empty vacant houses. WOW, how do you think that worked? I was able to help put in quite a few exceptions, so there wasn't a sign, for thieves, pasted on your front door—out of state thieves could just pick up the list of empty houses, online, before coming to Toledo.

No investor really has the time to fight all these battles; they just want to run their own businesses. The battles that investors have fought before are always a great learning experience when shared with all.

Another benefit of banding together as investors is the ability to bring the great tools they have discovered along the way.

Remember Tony, who offers apps every meeting, and Alyce, who is up to five discounts on Home Depot?

Not to mention Scott Whaley, coming from Texas to stream meetings across the country, live; and also, Judy, who goes to all the mastermind events to bring back to the local group; and Tammy, who gives a classroom at a moment's notice, to educate investors, a several dozen at a time.

Everyone may have their own specialty but is willing to bring it back and share it for the benefit of all!

Chipping Away

It seems almost impossible to stop a crazy law once the government has put one into motion. They always put some cute problem-saving title on the laws, like *Save the Children.*

Investors have wasted tens of thousands of dollars trying to take these offensive laws to the state supreme court. After those several long years of struggling, and big dollar costs of taking bad laws to the supreme court, only to be shut out with no hearing, it is a real waste. It seems a waste of time and energy.

The government always seems to remove it from the books on that particular hearing day; at which point, the state Supreme Court refused to hear the case at all. Then, a few months later, the government will put the bad law back on the books, hoping they already broke your bank. Of course, the government will be using your own tax dollars to pay their lawyers to fight against you.

I have actually had more luck with chipping away at the law. This can be done with inserts, corrections, or even definition changes for the better.

Our local Lead Paint Dust inspection went through years of constant changes and compromises. I lost count at twenty-three changes, before even hitting the activation date. Some changes were because what was written was impossible to enforce. Other items were really unworkable in the real world. Several changes were elimination of larger groups that were willing to sue. Some were exempted to be used as allies. Don't forget all the changes due to unintended consequences, such as saving a child but throwing a whole family out on the streets.

Another great example is the Vacant House Law that we mentioned earlier. Gee, how has that worked out? Is Toledo the first city in the nation to attain zero vacant houses within their borders? It has been eight years, and we're still waiting for that to happen.

Toledo was going to mandate a huge sign that could be read from the street on all empty houses, declaring them vacant. Second was an online list of all the vacant houses in the city. So now, thieves no longer had to sneak around; they could see their targets from the street.

Worse yet, if there wasn't enough local burglars, all out of state thieves could just pick up the list of vacant houses on their way into town.

Well, we were able to get about eight changes to the law and the definitions of a vacant house, in time to save the investors' properties. Some of the changes were exceptions:

i.   If the house was listed for sale
ii.   If the house was advertised for rent, with signage
iii. If the house was being rehabbed, and permits being pulled
iv.   If you had at least one of the utilities still turned on

Chipping away made this law a moot point for most investors.

I even fought the law that makes renting to more than three unrelated occupants illegal. I'm pretty sure that *family status* is a protected class under federal civil rights laws, where you are guilty and must prove innocence.

If you ask the city which law to follow, they say *theirs*, of course, and let civil rights try you. I don't think that even sounds sane!

Chapter 4

Workshops

Basic (more often than not) 101

Workshops are usually all day, or at least most of the day. They are set up to go further in depth on a subject that investors want to learn more about.

The ratio at a general meeting seems to run at one-third visitor or new investor, one-third seasoned investors who have been around for decades, and one-third of all the investors in between the two extremes.

More often than not, a large section of any real estate investor meeting is new, or a beginning investor, or new to several different kinds of investing. Even long time or advanced investors are knowledgeable in one style of investing, but know very little about other ways of investing. Investor workshops are a great way to delve into a more particular or different investor style that may interest you. Workshops are even about a new technique or a new twist that another investor has perfected.

Workshops 101

An investor 101 workshop can give you a general idea of the pros and cons of many different ways of investing in real estate. 101 Workshops are great decision makers as to what venue of real-estate investing to get into. It then usually delves a little deeper into an explanation of all the different variations of each particular method.   101 Workshops also go into depth of personality needed, money needed, experience needed, and time needed, to go into several different types of investing.

101 Workshops generally cover just the most common avenues of investing. They usually cover the basics of *Buy and Hold*, another name for Housing Provider and rentals. Coverage would include the pros and cons of this style of investing. It is often referred to as the Golden Rule of real estate. It is the *go-to* type of investing, for good economy, bad economy, or an economy that just cannot decide what to do. It can be the holding pattern while the economy changes, or just to give you time to decide what you want to do.

I have over seventy units, mostly single-family, and I have let the residents pay the mortgage for thirty years now. As soon as I figure out how to get my partner, Uncle Sam, out of my pocket, I might change my strategy.

Another common one would be *Fix and Flips*, which need contractor style rehab skills. This style also needs marketing know-how for a quick sale. This may be a good reason why I hold fourteen or more contracting licenses, and 2 real estate licenses as well. Nowadays, I would just join my local real estate investors association, and build a team with the discounted vendors members.

101 Workshops would also usually cover *Wholesaling*, also known as *bird dogging*. You would need a lot less money outlay, but you would need negotiating, contracts, and people skills. Usually, extra time is also a necessity.

The investor would be out looking for properties and deals, which the busier investors do not have time to do. It can be as simple as driving to different or desired areas as much as possible, looking for clues, such as high grass, a full mail slot, many newspapers piling up, a closed-up look, and no vehicles.

Communication skills come in with walking the area and talking with the neighbors, and finding the story that goes with that house. Take pictures of the condition and area, and start tracking the owner.

Once contact is made with the owner, negotiate a deal that you think would please an investor.

Now, the second hunt is for the buyer/investor that sees the potential that you did. Now it's time to negotiate again–this time with the investor/buyer.

Advanced 201

Advanced Workshops are also an excellent way to explode your real estate investing into many new directions. Instead of just the basic workshops, they can actually take you into a better understanding of many different ways of doing real estate investing. Many of these, you may not even be aware of.

Some are even just new and better ways to improve the ways you are already investing. It only takes one investor, using a new twist, to excite you into doing it the very next day in your own business. They turn out to be some of the best workshops.

Workshops can also advance the style of real estate investor you are currently doing, to the next level. This works especially well for tax advantages that you didn't know existed. Learning something new that you had no time to learn, is a bonus. There are wonderful ones, besides tax advantages, often called loopholes, or notes. There are different kinds and styles of notes in every area. I have noticed that note investors in our area travel to Indiana, etc., to pick up notes of an auction style.

Estate planning is needed by everyone, and sooner rather than later. One never knows how quick *later* can show up and knock on your door, and leave your family in the cold, without a clue about what investors really do. These experts can be brought in reasonably, if not free, just to be able to be in front of a group of investors.

Speaking of experts that really know their material, especially for investor self-directed IRAs, Roth IREAs, inherited IRAs, and 1031 exchanges, there is Equity Trust and CamaPlan. These are the ones I know of, because Dick Desich was the first to even do it as I know them today. Carl Fisher actually flew all the way in from China to teach the Toledo investors. What a time change that had to be after a fifteen hour flight.

Don't forget advanced money and finance, like creative investing, private lending, and much more. This is a topic all investors, including advanced seasoned ones, are searching out all the time.

Workshops can also help an investor decide whether or not to abandon the type of real estate investing they are already doing. Workshops can make you ready to change what you are currently doing, and switch to a whole new investing career.

Another great session for advanced investors is networking amongst themselves. These sessions can be done in a variety of ways also. Often, there are minimum requirements.

This can be the number of years you have been an active investor. It can be what your portfolio is worth. It can also be the variety of deals you have done, no matter how many years you have been in real estate investing. It could be by invitation only. Another might be your creativity in doing deals. With a few, the only requirement may be a large sum of money charged to keep smaller investors out.

The variety doesn't end with entrance requirements. Masterminds can be the sharing of how your deals were created. Some masterminds actually do deals together as a pool, or individually with each other. They can take place almost anywhere, and it can be the same location all the time—like a breakfast or a lunch.

They can be a set time schedule or a full weekend. Masterminds are as unusual as the great deals and alliances that come out of them.

Speed (Dating) Networking

There are even very simple mini workshops that expand your horizons instantly, such as speed networking. In one short session, you can learn to introduce yourself, then let people know what you do and what you're looking for, in fifteen seconds. That leaves the other quarter of the minute for you to listen to the person you're meeting, and determine their needs. In that half minute, you have learned to automatically put yourself out there to every person you meet as a real estate investor.

You also meet many investors, in most cases, enough to create your database of buyers, sellers, and lenders, or contractors, etc. This will be an important list of availability contacts for what you need in the future. Ask for a card, and always jot down on the back a few notes of what you learned about them during that chance meeting. To be able to get together in a room with hundreds of other investors may even make more relevant acquaintances, because they are all investors with a real profit center.

Most likely, you are introducing yourself to someone who can either educate you, solve your problems, or increase your profits. This, also, would be creating your database to start as a wholesaler, which we talked about earlier.

Let's talk a little bit about set up, logistics, and noise level. I like to give a heads-up notice, in the newsletter or eblast, so everyone can bring tons of business cards to hand out.

It can easily start at a regular meeting, with chairs set up in normal rows.

Instruct everyone in the rear section of the audience to stand and move forward, to fill in all the empty seats.

Walk up to the front or first row of investors, and ask them to stand. Once all have cooperated, have them grab their chairs and turn them to face the 2nd row, and have them sit back down, knee to knee. Now that everyone has the idea, go to every odd row—3, 5, 7, etc.

Have them repeat this by standing up, turning their chairs 180 degrees, and facing the people in front of them, knee to knee.

There is always a few shy ones but not for long.

The instructions are to create a 15-second intro to give directly across, then listen to the intro given back to you, and swap cards.

Then a bell/buzzer will sound every minute for row #1 to move one chair to the right and start all over again. Plus, the final person in the back comes up front.

Once it starts, it sounds like an auditorium on full blast.

The challenge is to get some of them to move. They have just met the person or deal they wanted, and want to keep talking to them. It's a full time job getting the person to move so the whole row can get to the next seat.

It's loud, it's chaotic, and it's a ton of fun, with a purpose.

The investors learned how to introduce themselves and tell what they do, quickly. They just did it, fifty to a hundred times, so now it is automatic, and they can do it in their sleep. Best of all, they met at least half of the investors in the room.

Fire Fire!

Investors, most often, are entrepreneurs too. It is challenging to keep them engaged unless it is new and interesting.

Every once in a while, I out-do all the past experiences.

One of our sessions was near the 4th of July holiday, so attendance was expected to be very low. As an entrepreneur, the decision was made to invite the fire marshal for an active onsite demonstration and training session.

I hunted down and located a service that would loan us as many full fire extinguishers as we wanted. The tough part was that we needed them for only one night, and we were going to use them all up.

We then went to the area's head Fire Marshal for permission, and to set up a live training session.

Getting the hall's permission was not the easiest either. We labeled it as a safety training, outside the building on the far edge of the parking lot.

I finally asked the hall rep, "You do want us to know how to use the fire extinguisher if there is ever a fire, don't you?"

The fire marshal arrived in full equipment and did an interesting training session. He then proceeded to set the parking lot on fire. He then personally taught every single investor there, one by one, how to correctly and quickly put out fires with fire extinguishers.

I was surprised to learn that you do the opposite of what your instincts are telling you. Some members got it right immediately, because you had to be aggressive and charge the fire. Others had to practice a little.

But all were successful in getting the fires out. The picture of the investors fighting the fires was fantastic, to the point of dramatic.

It was fantastic, but I will probably have a hard time trying to top that on any future July meetings.

For any of the workshops, I am also always searching out inexpensive venues. I'm usually checking out libraries, conference rooms, community rooms, etc. If you are lucky, one of the members has an extra room that can be commandeered for a class room. The intensive search is in order to keep all workshops affordable. It's all about the training and education, not the cost.

In order to keep the attendee present and in the workshop, I often provide a continental plus breakfast, and also lunch. Even this means scouring the local grocers at midnight so it can be done affordably. It also helps that my vice president owns Vito's Pizza, and gets a good deal on lunch.

It is set up for a good learning experience for all attendees, and keeps them in the room for the full session. This is important for the education, and for the speaker to get his whole message out.

It goes a long way to making every workshop, if not *on fire*, then at least the best it can be. Sometimes creativity and excitement by the speaker, the MC, and the volunteers will set the mood for learning.

PHP

Programming is one of the toughest committees and jobs for the investors meetings. It is never ending, and just keeps flowing from year to year. First, you have to struggle to find different topics so you do not repeat constantly. Then you have to find excellent experts in those topics, for a minimum of twelve monthly meetings. It also helps if those experts know how to speak and present their topic in an interesting and fun manner.

This is no small task, especially after thirty years of searching out new, exciting, and relevant programs. It helps to concentrate on the real estate building blocks that investors need to know. Add to that all the business basics that are necessary to run, and keep running, successfully. And don't forget, when a program is a real hit, and the investors keep asking for more, that is a winner that should be added to the schedule on an annual basis. They seem to be far and few in between, and even then they do seem to change throughout the decades.

The best ones we currently repeat throughout the years are only a few. I love having the spring Trade Fair. In our area, it is timed in April, when everyone is trying to break out of winter and get things going. It is a wonderful, party-like atmosphere that highlights all our great business partners. It is a way for the vendors to get the message out to investors and the public. It is also a way for the investors to collect all the great discounts, benefits, and savings for the whole year. I keep that Trade Fair newsletter, with all our business partners, on my van visor for the whole year.

The second popular program is our *Shark Tank investor style*, every fall. It highlights all the lenders. It actually teaches all the different kinds of lenders, and what they need to lend out money.

The third program that is repeated every year is our yearend Holiday Extravaganza. It is our time of the year to give back to our investor members and their families. It starts with a great buffet, then awards our wonderful volunteers, and highlights every board member (and volunteer). It also presents our grads for the year, and then presents for all, before the DJ starts.

Another repeat is the Mini Workshops. A lot of the smaller topics, or hands-on classes that may not fill a whole program, are splattered around the room in one Mini Workshop night. Even some of our vendors do a few workshops.

In our county, we have formed a relationship with the county auditor, Anita Lopez, and she brings the Board of Revision to the people! In our case, she will actually have the office at the back of our meetings, for investors to reduce their property taxes. I will cover this further in the book.

But what about all the rest of the many meetings?

The ultimate answer for investor education is PHP (Professional Housing Provider). I know the media and government officials only know the term, *landlord*, which they always use in a derogatory format.

One of the big bonuses of getting educated with other investors, is keeping the government from deciding they need to set your standards and provide education themselves. The Professional Housing Provider is similar to a two-year small business course, strictly in real estate investing. It covers as many as eighteen necessary topics, to make investors a successful business person and an investing professional.

This system is also a wonderful miracle for programmers trying to set meetings with the highest educational content. PHP would give you 18 months—a year and a half—of content, topics, and ideas that would not repeat for a year and a half.

The best programs I know were put together in Ohio, by Vena and the chosen by National REIA, as the best format they wished to use. They have grown, changed, and improved over the years.

Some of the main topics needed as basics were the ones I used for decades: management, purchasing, financing, local regs, insurance, fed regs, taxes, negotiating, appraisal, contract law, ethics, fair housing, marketing, landlord/tenant law, and rehab, to name a few.

This takes a great burden off the programmer's job. But most of all, it helps make a well-rounded investor that is going to be able to stay in business. Investing is a business and needs to be treated that way so it does not fail.

These topics are not the whole answer, but they give plenty of options to take all investors to their next level.

Now we have a variety of topics to choose from, and also the trying task of making them interesting and useful for your local area. Most of the presenters can actually come from your local area, for sure. Some of the best presenters are your own vendors and business partners.

Just having the knowledge in any one of those topics does not make a wonderful program automatically. I always request three things to start with: picture, bio, and outline of the presentation. After that, I will ask for any articles they may have on the topic, and the intro they suggest for the newsletter.

I need the picture, topic, and bio at least a month ahead of time in order to get it published, so that is a natural request. As soon as I get the outline, it goes through what I call the PHP process.

Let's take an example of insurance. An agent usually knows their own company policies, but I am looking for specific policies that pertain to real estate investors. Normally, the outline has topics, and they include auto and life insurance type policies. I will work with the agent and ask for a substitute of pet, vacant, and rehab instead. It has to be all about what a real estate investor needs and has a hard time finding for a reasonable price. Now, I not only have a better presenter but a better program, and success for both the agent and the investor.

The best of all, with the PHP (professional housing program), is that every one of our meetings and workshops have been certified on a PHP topic, and you will get a certificate at the end of each session.

This will lead to PHP graduates that you can award at your meetings, or at your holiday or end of the year program. It also encourages members to stay with you a minimum of two years to earn their PHP. The graduate investor can then add Professional Housing Provider to their business cards–WIN-WIN for all!

Board of Review

Another great workshop is inviting the county auditor or the Board of Review–the ones that reduce property taxes. I invite the county auditor, Anita Lopez, in as a speaker, yearly, to teach about investors' tax bases, and general information investors need to know. She is a great speaker and really engages with the audience, and answers their questions.

At our original meetings with Anita, the auditor, the light bulb went off. I finally asked the ultimate question one year, and we exploded from there. With the auditor on stage, we cornered her: "Why are taxes rising every year even though property values are seriously dropping with the real estate crash?" The answer was simple and straight forward, but it was a bombshell. *The auditor department has no ability or protocol to reduce anyone's taxes. It can only be reduced by request of the tax payer.* What an eye opener. From then on, I have been able to assist hundreds of investors to reduce their property taxes.

I keep the current yearly form on hand for any investors that need it. Taking it one step further, I invite the auditor and the board of revision, every January, February, and March, to our monthly investor meeting. In our county system, those are the months that you can contest your taxes from the previous year.

They actually now bring the whole office, computers, and staff to our investor meetings, and set up several tables at the back of the room. The auditor's staff spends the evening taking investor claims to reduce their property taxes. The most recent reduction proclaimed by an investor was a refund check for $9000-plus. Yeah!

As with any new task, once you actually do it, the fear and uncertainty is gone, and repetition is easier. Once you have reduced your property taxes at a friendly meeting of investors, going on to repeat in following years is easy.

As a matter of fact, the toughest part of the *tribunal* hearing is keeping the investor from bragging about their property. This is not the time, nor place, to tell all the good things you have done to the property. I have actually had to kick investors under the table to stop bragging. BOR property review is the place to enumerate the deficiencies of the property.

Once you have thoroughly covered all the short comings, then it is time to denounce the bad surroundings of boarded up, vacant, fire damaged, demos, and graffiti ridden units. Don't stop there; follow up about gangs, shootings, fires, and whatever applies from the local news, in your particular area of town.

The most important point of any education is the ongoing effect that expands throughout your business.

Do not forget the financials, because they will ask. The Board of Revision are non-investors, and see the grass as greener on the other side. They may refer to you as a guru, or bigger pockets who pay their salaries, even if they don't say it out loud.

So, just like tenants, don't expect them to understand your business or financials. If they ask about your rental income, be sure to give an approximate estimate of what the monthly rent is *supposed* to be, because seldom is rent always complete and on time. Remember to qualify how many months the property was vacant, late, unpaid, and partial paid. Be sure to mention the property expenses also, such as taxes, insurance, mortgage, sewer, water, lawn care, evictions, and management, to name a few.

It is only fair to give the whole picture, including damages, foreclosures, and evictions. This is the time to talk about your worst tenant horror stories. After all, you are just trying for a fair tax so you are able to put your resources back into the property.

Chapter 5

Pothole Filler - Fantastic, Cool Contract Clauses & Addendum

Rules of the Road (Lease is Law to resident, but seldom in the court)

Networking with other investors, popped up a bunch of ways to perfect my leases and contracts. When I start talking about addendums, the first question I always get is, "Is that legal?" My primary concern with a lease is that the tenant knows that these are the rules of the property. What they are reading in the lease is the law for them, not necessarily in the courts. Luckily, in my forty-two years, I've never had a lease go to court, except for eviction. On the other hand, I never knowingly added anything to my lease that I thought was not legal.

There are plenty of guidelines and rules to follow. Start with federal. That would be civil rights and fair housing—not quite the same. Fair housing often is local, and most hire testers. The new hot point is ads that say *no pets*.

The 2nd layer of rules, rights, and regulations would be the state level. So far, every state that I have checked has a set of landlord/tenant laws. Most of them are very vague, and it is pretty easy to stay within the generalities. Most seem to be health and safety, followed with paperwork requirements.

Often, they do not give you the *forms* needed, but just mention what should be included on the forms. Some are specific enough to mention size of the lettering on the forms.

As a group of Toledo investors, we created a county eviction notice, which the courts have now been accepting for over thirty years. Having the form ready-made takes a lot of the liability off the shoulders of each individual investor, because we share for FREE. So, unless they start changing Ohio landlord/tenant law, we are good to go.

I should mention that there are very exact specifics about the resident's security deposit. Last time I looked, if you collected more than the rent, then separate accounts, interest rates, and rules may apply. Also, if return is not one hundred percent, it needs to be itemized. PLEASE add a few **no charges**, or the judge will be deciding wear and tear, not you.

A few bonuses on Security Deposits:

i.   Most important, the resident must provide a forwarding address to send it to.
ii. You do have 30 days to assess damage and estimate prices.
iii. If not by 30 days, penalty can double or triple the down payment in court (send with proof of mailing).
iv. If you use bonus, not late fee, it can be added into damages.
v.   If you don't serve 2nd cause (damages) at the same time, there is no successful service.

An excellent practice in any area would be to get to court early and watch all the cases. You will get a feel for what the Judge likes or doesn't like, and how he reacts to both sides. It will be invaluable information for your hearing when it is called.

One annoying problem is when the housing provider calls and asks what to do about their tenant.

My standard answer: Read your own lease. If nothing is there, make sure it's in the new one.

Another continual problem is that the tenant won't let you in, for which I give the same standard answer.

You shouldn't be asking permission; you should be just

giving them *notice of entry*, noting when the inspections will take place, and if they cannot be present, then you, the management, will be there.

If the locks are changed, they leave you a key, or you enter anyhow, and change the locks back. This is completely allowed by my landlord law, so please check yours.

These days, I have asked to text notice of entry. They do have to put some sort of answer text back so I know they received the notice. If they do not acknowledge the text, I will post a note on the door and return the next day.

1st is a Mistake, 2nd is a Fault

Subject to the landlord tenant rules in your area, it never hurts to have everything spelled out specifically. Every time you take a big fall from a *professional* tenant, it needs to be added to your lease so it doesn't happen again.

Every time the government adds a new crazy law, add a stop gap to your lease. I also feel very strongly that the first time things go wrong, it's a mistake. The second time, you need to take the blame, if you haven't corrected the problem within your lease.

First, a quick mention of the application. In case you are still doing it on paper, I have finally upgraded to doing it on the cell phone or by email address. If still doing it yourself on paper, several Fair Housing and Privacy act changes need to be noted. Signatures by renters need to be on a separate page because, when checking any of the application facts, you cannot send any of their private information—just their signature under the disclaimers, disclosures, and permission to check out what they have filled in.

Also, remember, if denying a tenant on any credit info, there are federal rules, letters, and free reports that you must follow through by sending to the applicant. I am lucky enough to use *RentPerfect*, a national private detective service that takes on all that responsibility and legality, and keeps us out of prison. They do not charge us, and their membership for a REIA group of investors is a ridiculous ninety-five cents. Check with NationalREIA.org. Not only due diligence, but *RentPerfect* then offers my renter a five dollar rental insurance, which is mandatory in my lease. PLUS, the policy has my name on it also!

When the rent is stated in the lease, it is also spelled out that all charges, fees, penalties, etc. are paid first, before their payment is used towards the rent. For instance, if the yard care has become a problem, a note is posted on the house. They will have till the weekend to take care of the problem before a crew is sent on the weekend to fix the problem, and the cost will paid by the occupant, to be paid prior to, or at the time of rent. It will be deducted from rent payment prior to being put towards the rent.

The quick track, or maybe I should say quicker track, through the court system when needed, is always nonpayment of rent.

This is the major key to getting all corrections or problems actually taken care of.

Too many people in the house that are not on the lease? $100 each for anyone not on the lease, retroactive to the beginning of the lease, if not reported by the resident. All occupants over the age of eighteen must be on the lease.

Unregistered *pets*? $50 deposit and $50/month per pet. If not added to the lease by the resident, then retroactive back to the beginning of the lease. Lost your key for the 2nd, 3rd, or 4th time? $25 replacement or locksmith fee.

If locks are changed without a key copy to management, full change fee will be charged to occupant. With or without copy of the keys, I do not allow any lock changes because we use *LandLord locks*. One master key for all 100+ properties, and one change key, means I never have to change a doorknob again. Google it! It is a fantastic company, and the same price as doorknobs off the shelf of any big box store.

Hopefully, you see a pattern here. The quick track, or maybe I should say quicker track, through the court system when needed, is always nonpayment of rent.

Speaking of extra people in the unit, how about a *roommate agreement?* I hardly ever see the same last names anymore on the leases. Roommate agreements clearly state that every individual in the unit owes the full rent, and how they split payment amongst themselves has nothing to do with you. All rent is payable when due, and a partial payment is accepted but will not stop eviction paperwork.

All charges, fees, or corrections always attach back to the money—the rent. It's all about being able to take it to the eviction court for nonpayment of rent. In our county, that is the only quicker path through the court system.

Red Tagged

One of the things that can drive an investor crazy is no control over the utilities that residents have in their own name. Some utility companies now have a manager program, where the owner will at least get a notice when they are being disconnected. This is critically important in severe weather.

A couple of additions to the lease I have seen are things such as red tag addendum, making the renter responsible if his utilities get turned off, and testing causes red tagged furnaces and water heaters.

For some, tenants seem to get their utilities turned off a lot. Whether it's for a gas leak, for nonpayment, or just saving money during the summer, it causes unintended consequences and damage. It makes sense to have your lease spell out what happens if your mechanicals get red tagged by the utility companies. If the problem is caused because the utilities were suddenly shut off, and now they have to test the lines in order to turn them back on, it makes sense that the additional expense will be paid by the occupant who failed to keep the utilities on (as per the lease). Otherwise, the behavior is sure to be repeated.

An addendum would go something like this:

Resident is responsible for payment of all utilities, to include water, sewage, garbage collection, cable TV, electricity, gas, local telephone service—even if the bills remain in Management's name. Failing to pay the utility bills will be interpreted as a default and a violation of this Agreement. Any installation costs, and **red tags or repairs due to turn-offs,** are the responsibility of Resident. Any wall jacks, telephone, or cable installation shall remain with the Property.

Besides red tag problems, it also covers the utilities that are not in the resident's name. In our local area, the water company is owned by the city, and is rough to work with. One of the water company's stipulations is that the water, sewer, and trash stay in the owner's name.

Clauses like this cover all utilities used by the occupant. As you can see, it does not matter whose name they are in. I quite often find different names on their other utility bills. Also, one of the basics I learned early on, from my fellow investors, was to never turn over keys to any property till you have the confirmation numbers from the local utility companies.

Bedbugs

When we talk about expenses and big losses, this topic floats to the top of the pile every time. It seems to be a plague rapidly spreading throughout the Midwest, then coast to coast. I hear it asked about in whispers, with fear in their voices.

There seems to be no real cure for the bedbug epidemic, and you can see mattresses put outside every neighborhood you drive through.

It always puzzles me, though, to see mattresses or couches stacked up alongside the exterior wall of the house or porch. Really? If this critter was the reason, then why have it against the property? I would have it as far away as possible. It seems you would toss it to the street curb for pick up and removal.

Bedbugs are a very frightening, nationwide problem on its own, without the legal repercussions. Occupants automatically assume that they came from the house and not from their used furnishings and visiting friends. Bedbugs do not come from empty houses; they travel with people, visitors, and used furnishings.

The bedbug addendum inserted into my lease makes it very clear that it is the occupant's responsibility for due diligence. Obviously, when the problem arises, the occupant is ready to blame the house and owner; but, for some reason, they are seldom motivated to follow the strict directions on what needs to be done to cure the problem.

Truly, having them follow the detailed instructions of taking care of all their possessions is paramount, along with their cooperation to clean up your property. I am planning to share some of these great addendums on www.AnnaMillsPRO.com.

The Bedbug Addendum makes the renter, who brought the bedbugs, responsible financially, and to follow all rules needed to correct the problem.

I keep it under pest control. The resident agrees to provide any pest control as needed. Under no circumstances shall the landlord and/or agents of the landlord be held responsible for any of the tenant's losses, damages, or expenses, including special, consequential, or punitive, arising out of a pest infestation, inspection, or treatment.

Additionally, the tenant agrees to indemnify and hold harmless the landlord, it's agents, and employees, from any action, claims, losses, damages, and expenses, including but not limited to attorney's fees that the landlord may incur as a result of a bedbug infestation, inspection, or treatment. Failure to promptly report pests, and failure to comply with treatment instructions, or any other violations of any other provisions of this addendum shall be a violation of the residential lease agreement. Said violations and breaches constitute grounds for eviction, and/or termination of occupancy; and/or subjects the tenant to all other damages, costs, legal fees, and expenses, as stated in your lease and/or this addendum.

You may never get entangled in any of these issues, but it is agreed to by each of the parties as to what happens if these expensive things do occur.

A couple of additions to the lease I have seen, other than red tag addendums and bedbug addendums, are multi-unit, students, *I'm not your parent* addendums, multiple residents addendums, etc.

Multi Unit (not your parent)

Multi units are a world of their own. To me, it is a totally different kind of investing than single family homes.

The bonus is many separate incomes. If some don't pay, there are still many that keep your income streaming in monthly. With a good portfolio, it also opens you up to qualifying for commercial loans.

On the other side of the coin, it mixes together a diverse pool of people, not just families, as in single family houses. Just as not all families get along, multi-unit mixtures can go crazy also.

It can become hands-on intensive if you try to micromanage every little episode that goes on in your units on a daily basis. I have learned to be very clear with the residents, right up front. I disclose that I am not their parent. I even put signs on the property that say:

"If it's important enough to report, report it to the police; if not, work it out yourselves."

Another great reminder is:

"Anything left in the public halls, consider it public property; it will be removed."

Other investors are a wealth of knowledge and real-life experiences. Sometimes it is the simple day-to- day problems.

Mike Butler taught me how to get three-year leases consistently. It was so simple. He said, "Just ask for it." How could that possibly work? It really depended on how he asked for the three-year lease that was so genius.

"Would you like to lock your rent price in for one, two, or three years?"

My three year's lease numbers jumped by more than fifty percent, thanks to Mike's entrepreneurship and willingness to share.

Do you notice that almost everything these days has become disposable? People must buy their clothing at the dollar store. When I enter for a repair, clothes are knee deep. I stand still and look confused, and just wait. Instead of offering to move or clean up the mess, they just instruct me: "Oh, just walk over the top of them to get to the repair!"

What?

Move out time was no better. I almost needed a dumpster because they took what they wanted and left the rest. Lou Brown had this cute little *Move-Out Cleaning* letter. I have to admit that the letter did include, step-by-step, what and how to clean. But the real gem was at the bottom, when he tied all the steps back to getting their deposit returned. Wow, it really worked. I was amazed to now walk into some of my houses all cleaned and even vacuumed.

There's a lot of these great tips you can learn, just from being in a group of other investors. I know one investor who checks interior housekeeping on his properties every month. Other investors only worry about it when they get them returned, and do the rehab then. Some investors use late fees; others use early pay bonuses. On-time-pay bonuses are used to cure the problem for which most courts will not award late fees.

Multiplying Residents

Ever stop by your properties and have no idea who is answering the door? Or try to figure out the mystery of the doubling water bill, when only 1 adult and 1 child are on the lease? Does it seem like a revolving door or a family reunion every day?

Investor addendum can be specific about occupancy and how many adults are in the house. In some areas, it is important to know all adult occupants; in case of eviction, all must be named.

Occupancy addendum helps enforce who is on the lease and who is occupying, in case the number doubles. This adds a stop gap that says all adults 18 or over must be on the lease.

If the adult additional occupant is not reported, it is $100 a month per extra adult. That is retroactive back to the beginning of the lease. Again, in all areas, everything should be tied back monetarily, because the *quickest* eviction process is usually non-payment of full rent. Of course, all fines and fees will be deducted from payment prior to being applied to the rent.

Here's some sample wording showing what I am referring to:

The Property shall be occupied by the undersigned **1 adult and 1 child(ren) only,** as named in the original application. Guests staying over 14 days will be considered in violation, and additional monthly rent of $100.00 per person shall be due, chargeable from the beginning date of this Lease.

Resident shall be responsible and fully liable for the conduct of all guests.

Also, in multi families, residents do not own the yard, common areas, patios, parking, etc. Therefore, residents need to keep close reins on their pets, kids, vehicles, and equipment. These areas belong to all, and must be treated as any local park. This includes immediately picking up after your pets and kids, just as if you are on the public sidewalk.

Multi units, in our area, quite often are on the verge of trash cans vs commercial size dumpsters. So be sure to check the local rules where you are. I have disappearing trash cans all the time.

The current process, if you need replacements, is a formal police report taken out.

Thanks to investors, neighbors, and cell cameras, we now know over five hundred are being dumped by the trash trucks themselves, with zero effort to retrieve them out of the trucks.

Wow, social media and cameras are at everyone's fingertips.

There are great, thorough, info-based speakers on multi units, like Anthony Chara, to bring in for unbelievable training and collaborating.

You can learn so much from other investors that just energizes your business all over again.

Chapter 6

Successful Trainers/Topics

Teachers vs. Speakers

I respect experts in their field, and loved to bring them in to talk with the local investors. Even though networking with each other is invaluable, bringing someone specializing in different hot topics, which has perfected a system, is always a bonus.

I really like to start by explaining to investors, or the whole audience, the difference between a teacher vs. a speaker. Both give excellent information and can educate you. Hopefully, sharing into that will take your business to the next level, or put a new money-saving/money-making twist to it also.

But with teachers, just like back in school, you better learn how to take really good notes about the topic—and not only take really good notes, but you have to be able to find those notes when you really need them. So, maybe you should index them for the important points you will need later. Plus, you need to be able to read those notes and remember what you meant at the time.

On the other hand, the speaker has not only learned the information he's presenting, but he is willing to teach you the tips and tricks that he has learned through the years. It does not stop there. A speaker usually has also created a system to be put in place. He has taken the time to transcribe it all, and put it in a book form, often with all the forms, and sometimes with audio and video. A speaker then wrapped it all in a package, had it published, and is willing to share it all with you.

It is something ready-made to put on your office shelf, to be handy and ready when you need it for any problems that pop up.

Even though he gives you up to ninety percent, and tons of content while teaching, you may want more. If the speaker has already created it, instead of doing it all yourself, you can have it right away.

I try to stress the fact that if you like what you hear, go for it, and make it your own at your office. If not, then gather what info you can while listening, and move on. There is no pressure either way.

PS: If a speaker indeed has a product to sell that you thought was good enough to buy, DO NOT stand in front of them and ask someone else to share the product price, and that you will make them a *copy* of it. Not only is this against copy write laws, it is stealing, and unethical in a lot of ways.

It happens all the time without people even thinking about what they are saying.

Not that I have ever sold anything; I am one of those teachers you have to take a lot of notes with. I have been told to slow down and not talk so fast, and that it's like trying to drink from a firehose.

Location, Location, Location

Bringing in the big national speakers is fine and exciting, and educational. Their presentations are not only informational but well-practiced and fun to listen to. Their message is entertaining and packaged perfectly. They are definitely good presenters, as well as educators.

By being in your location, the local speakers and teachers are quite often the best fit. Their knowledge and education is fine tuned to the local needs and the local laws. It is still often necessary to fine tune their knowledge and education a little more to the specific real estate investor format.

In order to do that, I request an outline at the same time that I get their bio and picture. I ask this of all presenters, before being added to our program listing. This includes speakers, large and small, and our vendor members also.

An outline of what they're going to cover as their educational piece can be used to make small adjustments to fit the real estate investors' mode. This gives me an opportunity to help them tweak their presentation to better fit the local investor. Even national and international speakers are happy to get feedback of what local laws may affect what they are about to present. No one wants to find out afterwards about local laws that may change what they are teaching. For instance, I would hate to have a creative sign company in if signs are illegal in your area.

This adjustment should make both the speaker and the investor quite satisfied by the time the program has concluded. It also prepares the presenter for the questions that will come from the investors at the conclusion.

Location is a great tool to bring into specialty topics regarding the obstacles investors face locally that may not be a problem elsewhere. That is why there are local chapters, because real estate has always been about location, location, location. That really holds true for real estate investors as well, and just as much for education as for buying and selling.

Our local authorities bring a wealth of information. They are not always the most exciting or practiced speakers, but they know and live their topics. Some may even feel like the enemy, like taxes and inspectors. But you know what? The info they bring makes investors more aware of the ins and outs. Sometimes you need to know them so you can find the hidden trails in between. Often, it is the things they don't say that turn out to be the most important gems.

There are two important things. First, just bringing them in, where they feel like they know you as the ones who want to learn, is a great breakthrough. For instance, do you know why Walmart has those greeters? No, not because they want to employ the elderly—because they reduce shoplifting by 80%, by having eye-to-eye contact with someone when they enter. Really!

So, here's your chance to break the barrier of just being a name: a *picky inspector*, or a *cheap-fix* investor. Now you are somebody that they know and have met. It's a little less easy to be a jerk, on both sides. After all, your group just gave them their one day of fame as a featured speaker for the month.

Second, I mentioned what they do not say. What are their quirks and hot buttons? What things do you make sure are always exactly current, and what things don't matter? What is their personality? Do they want to talk for five minutes, or do they want you to be ready and quick, so they can get to their next appointment? Also, ask them questions directly, to know what and how they personally want things done.

I actually take my licenses mandatory continuing education from the inspectors' classes at the local union hall. Now, I am neither an inspector nor union, but I know how they think and how they are going to interpret any new laws, and how they want the work done. Bingo!

Vendor Topics

Surprisingly, some of the greatest presentations are from our business or vendor members themselves. All 4 of our business memberships are really complete marketing packages.

All the different levels include a minimum of 4 FREE tables at our live main meeting, and unlimited at both our one-on-one Wednesdays and Friday breakfast meetings. They also have four FREE ads in our Investor Survival Journal newsletter. They can plan to use their ads the same month they have a table at the meeting, or the opposite months, to spread out their exposure. Also, they have a FREE table at the huge annual Trade Fair every spring.

More membership levels: more ads and exposure. We also have a sponsorship level, where we provide the table cover with their design and logo. Plus, they get a seven-foot pop-up sign of their company design and logo.

On top of that, we have a two-page list of sponsorships that business partners can add to their membership.

All businesses must be members to participate and advertise at our meetings. I learned a long time ago that business will not remember investors, and investors will not remember your business, unless you are around for a while and participating,

Business partners get to have their picture and logo flashed onto the screen all during the networking. An advanced idea in the working is a 15-second commercial, on stage before the main speaker, if time permits, to keep their benefits in front of the investors.

Many business partners have increased their exposure by offering gift cards, or little *extras* for coming and joining them at their individual tables. Investors' time is very precious, even at a meeting, but I want to make sure they get the most out of their time as well.

Business partner topics include actually doing *hands-on* sessions that show the investors how rehab works. This has included things as big as showing how easy refrigerator repair is. Another success is the simplicity of vinyl window installation, with only four screws, a level, and some insulation.

Business partners showing how to use their product, or the correct way their product or service is used to the best benefit, is another winner. Our vendor members are a wonderful source of education. This education goes a long way to educate, and is often remembered the longest.

Whenever there is an actual hands-on session that involves the investors, it is a bonus on both sides. Investors truly remember those business partners, what they have to offer, and the benefits they gain.

Business partners on in-depth investor topics are also great to widen all investors' vision and knowledge of the variety that is out there. They are also great teachers for all-day workshops, so the investor that is interested can get fully prepared to actually invest in that style of real estate.

Live events, like *bus tours* or *cool tools* are educational but also fun and memorable as hands-on. Topics can be widespread to include investor incomes that are large and small.

Bus tours are popular for many different reasons. They help show in real time what is being done in your own neighborhoods. It can be a rehab bus tour showing all different stages of progress. It can also show all different styles done by different investors in different areas. Tours can point out the different rehab styles for a sale vs. that for a rental. Another tour would be about how to inspect the house before you buy it, learning also how to estimate repair costs as you go.

How about a tour right at a Home Depot, with one of their hand-on training classes? I also like to call in Mr. Rehab, Pete Youngs, for both his Rehab Bus Tour and also his unusual Cool Tools sessions.

Investing and investor education should always be fun and entertaining. Our general meeting is the 2nd Tuesday of every month, and it starts at 6:30 pm. Many investors come right from a full day of work or investing. The point is you have to be able to keep them awake, keep them interested, and have a little fun— they won't learn anything when they're bored to death.

Splatter Method

The splatter method of education involves speakers, teachers, vendors, and workshops. This helps the investors get a true flavor of all the different methods out there, including education, benefits, discounts, partners, and much more. Diversity in education prepares an investor for all economies.

This splatter method of real estate investing expands investors in the many different ways of real estate investing. Diversity in real estate can make a great portfolio, but it needs a lot of education to back it up.

You can learn several different ways to get into and out of real estate investing, no matter what the economy is doing.

I am always looking for win-win situations between the educator and the investor, as well as between the individual investors themselves.

Great topic headings are always starting with the basics needed for any business, such as marketing, purchasing, financing, local regulations, tax implications, negotiating, management, and insurances. I covered more of that earlier with PHP, Professional Housing Providers.

One of the sensitive areas I have always been very careful with is mentoring. It can backfire both ways. A great mentor can be beat down by a student that has no respect for the teacher's time. Calls during Christmas dinner or any private time is over the top. On the flip side, a mentor that takes advantage of newer investors' time and money is unforgiveable. After decades of not using mentoring systems, I finally ran across a way for it to work safely in our area.

There is a speaker, Tony Youngs, who has a mentoring program that I found wonderful. He actually comes to your town for the student, new or not. He starts at the court house and sticks with the student till he gets his first property done! I was not only impressed with his mentoring done successfully, but relieved at the professionalism and safety I saw.

So, to date, that is the mentoring program I have used so far for those investors that want a step by step starter.

I try to keep all education rounded from basic to advanced, covering as many topics similar to a small business course, strictly in real estate investing. Also added in are all the new latest rages or twists that make investing even more profitable.

Income Methods - Large vs. Small

There are *so* many ways to participate in real estate investing. As a matter of fact, when you get right down to it, every one of the investors does it a little bit different–their own way. You can learn from every one of them, even if it's how you don't want to do it.

Smaller

Housing providers, buy and hold, or basically renters, have always been considered the golden rule for any economy. You are letting the renter pay your mortgage for the next number of decades that it takes till paid off.

They are also known as *get rich slow* style, for those that just want the steady monthly income. They want the deductions against their own income. They want to get to a lower or zero tax bracket. They want to collect those extra checks every month.

They are great members for business and investor members. Housing Providers always need stuff because it gets broken on a daily basis. Plus, they are always looking for more houses from other investors, and they don't have to be perfect. Sharing tenant phone calls when your units are full is another great advantage.

Larger

There are plenty of other investing methods that are more of a business than investing, such as the wholesaling, rehabbing flips, and flipping. I refer to them as businesses because all of them stop producing income when you stop working.

Rehabbing can be flips or buy and hold. For rehab flips, you have a tight ratio of time and money between purchase price, rehab costs, holding costs, and sale price. Do not forget to figure in time, economy, and Uncle Sam in your wallet pocket as a partner. Yes, capital gain taxes can be as high as a fifty percent partner, depending on your income and tax shelters. Just remember to figure it all in to the pot of money up front. In other words, the key is, as always, to make your money on the purchase. That lump sum may not seem so large when shared with the tax man.

This is where an investor group is so handy. Getting a free CMA (current market analysis) from a local realtor member would help. Also helpful is construction members sharing some of the current building material and labor increases. Or even end up with new or better, or less expensive, methods to cure the problems of your purchase house. They can even come up with the knowledge to repair problems you think cannot be overcome.

There are always plenty of examples of all investing methods in a group of investors.

All methods of real estate investing should be welcome, and are a great benefit to the group as a whole. The successful ones that have created a business out of it are usually more than happy to share with other members.

Which is better? Which is really larger or smaller–the 70 checks each month, with tons of deductibles, or the lump sum, with the tax man looking over your shoulder?

What's your background? What are your talents? What are your connections? Ask your tax expert.

Hopefully, he is a member of the local investors association, and specializes in investor taxes. If not, ask him to join, or go to your huge pool of investors, and ask who they use and how long they have been at zero tax bracket.

Systems Set to Win-Win

Investors are always looking for systems that make it easier to reproduce a successful real estate method. That is when it becomes a career.

Another great point about learning from experts is, more often than not, speakers have the systems put into place. What they've already created is a way you can have a win-win, to solve and prosper by their info. You only have to decide if it is right for you.

Another way to have a win-win is to start to give back. The more involved you are, and the more you volunteer, the more you win back yourself.

It costs absolutely nothing to volunteer, except your time. So, if you are going to a meeting anyhow, why not use that time actively and multiply your return. As important as the education program, at any investor meeting, is the investor in attendance.

Imagine being an investor and brand new at your first meeting. How about being brand new about learning to invest? How better to multiply your knowledge and engagement than by volunteering to assist.

Volunteering to put up signage creates a tangible knowledge of the great business partners and benefits on each one of the signs. Also, short people, like me, will love you because it is a job they cannot reach.

Volunteering at the visitor table to sign new people in forms a bond with all the other new ones in the room. Telling them where everything is located and what will be happening during the meeting will educate you on the layout and what the scoop is.

Volunteer to assist at the members' registration, and meet all the long-term investor members and attendees. You will automatically start matching their faces and specialties, with their names.

Volunteer at the hospitality table. Besides the obvious benefits of food and drink, you will be where investors hang around and talk. You will be at the table where the surveys are filled out on the topics the local investors want to hear and learn more about. You will also be the first to see their open real estate comment on the back of the surveys.

Volunteer with the audio person, and choose some of the cool upbeat music running behind scenes at the meeting. Learn the microphone care and sound system. Watch firsthand and up close how we stream our meeting all over the country. Last month, we were in CA, NY, TX, LA, TN, and Perrysburg. Learn the other amazing businesses investors run also.

Volunteer to assist with the Orientation Sessions. You will get proficient in all the dozens and dozens of great benefits we have across the nation, not just local.

Volunteer to assist on the real estate bus tours and workshops to take your knowledge to the next level.

Learn the systems that run a real estate meeting, and you will expand your own real estate investor network. But more importantly, it will drive home the reality that systems can run your whole real estate investing career.

WIN-WIN volunteering will expose you to investors that have put into place some of the best systems there are.

It is the only way I could possibly balance two real estate offices, two construction companies, 14 licenses, over seventy rental properties, AND still have the time and commitment to volunteer to run Toledo REIA and National REIA.

Chapter 7

Shark Tank

Rules of the Sea

Real estate Shark Tank is a presentation we learn from investor sessions at National REIA events. It turned out to be a great solution for hooking investors up with the money they need.

Shark Tank, Real Estate Style, is where local *Sharks* (seasoned investors with cash in hand) will fight for the opportunity to buy your property or do a deal with you at the Shark Tank meeting!

The Toledo REIA version is for **fun, entertainment, and valuable learning opportunity**. Witness real life investing decisions of many of the biggest investors in Toledo. Put together your financial portfolio for ANY lender!

At our Shark Tank meeting, Toledo REIA will have our very own version of the smash hit, *Shark Tank*: fun entertainment and valuable learning opportunity. Witness real life investing decisions from some of the biggest investors in the city.

It also fills the gap and becomes an educational key for all different types of investors.

I am happy to share the complete *Rules of the Sea* I used to make our *Shark Tank, Real Estate Style* event successful. The underlying education is for the shark bait/investor to put together a successful portfolio that he could present to any money lender in the future.   But it is also to create the awareness that every lender wants something different, and to create a portfolio that is in tune with each particular lender.

Participants wanting to be funded need to fill out the Shark Tank registration and provide as much information as possible. We generally need their picture, their bio, and as much info and pictures about the deal as possible. The reason this is so important is because we want to involve the investors in the audience as well.

All the info provided to me will be on the overhead wall to share step-by-step on the screen as the deals go along.

Diversity in Sharks

Our first components, of course, are the sharks or the lenders in your area, or amongst your own investors.

Toledo REIA chooses *Sharks*–seasoned investors with the capability to act and close quickly! Each *Shark* has a different investing specialty, to buy, partner, or fund deals that participants bring to the table, if they deem it to be a good deal and accept your terms.

There are many species of sharks, for many types of deals.

There are the commercial lenders, the banks, the credit unions, the private lenders, the hard money lenders, private money lenders, the self-directed IRAs, and many more. Each one of these lenders has their own product, along with their own rules and needs.

The whole point of being a shark lender is getting your company or institution's information out in front of a room full of repeat investors. Talk about a targeted audience of repeat buyers.

This is the time that they can show investors that there are many different ways to do a deal. I try to use only our business member partners. If there's a great lender, then I approach them with the benefits of joining our investors association, to have a pool of clients that keeps doing deals repeatedly.

It is important that they know their own financial programs well, and how they can stretch them for non-owner occupied dwellings. They need to know all the addendums, exceptions, and bonuses available that may be unknown to the public.

Next, it sure helps if they can be interesting and fun while they explain how their programs work for investors. They need to be concise and explanatory of why a deal will or will not work for their company. Then they should be able to offer a way that it may work for them; then give their yes or no decision.

Sharks must also be able to supply their picture, bio, and company info. These will be used in the newsletter, advertising, and on the overhead during the meeting.

Any articles donated would be a great bonus for the newsletter or handouts.

Extra Shark Bait

The second needed component, of course, is the shark bait– the investors looking for funding for many different reasons. An investor might want equity out of his rental property, or they may want a partner to work with them on an upcoming deal; oh, and they might need an equity line to do many future deals.

The deals are as diverse as the investors. The goal is to make it educational and eye-opening to all the investors present. The second goal is to acquaint the lenders with the variety of the deals out there, and to form a relationship with the local pool of investors. The third goal is to educate the presenters that they can put together a portfolio good enough for any lender, when tweaked.

I put out a flyer called Participation Application & Instruction, with all the basics.

Toledo REIA chooses seasoned investors who all have the capability to act and close quickly!

Who Can Participate?

Toledo REIA actively takes submissions from all dues paying investor members. If not a member, you can JOIN as an investor member, and be eligible.

A maximum of 6 participants will be chosen by the Shark Tank committee, based on criteria below, and on a first-come basis. Each applicant can only submit ONE DEAL for consideration.

If an investor wishes to get on the show and submit one of their deals to the Sharks, to buy, partner, or fund....please follow the instructions for submission, below.

STEP 1: Submission Instructions
Submission deadline: 1st of the month, at noon
Submit to: www.AnnaMillsPRO@.com

Application basics should include:
- Property address
- ARV
- Purchase price
  - fund requested
  - or partnership proposition
- Repair price
- Picture of property
- What your DEAL is (partner, fund, equity, etc.)
- Proof of equity in the property????????????????
- name, telephone, address, email, bio, photo

No application will be reviewed for consideration until/unless EVERYTHING is submitted by the stated time.

STEP 2: Presentation Preparation
Once accepted as one of the official Shark Bait, your work is NOT over.

Property Photos: Submit your own photos of the property (max of 20) in digital format.
Presentation: Average is 4-6 minute presentation, with 6-8 minutes for questions by the Sharks. Address and pictures will be broadcast on the screen.

Presentation Outline:

* Offer: Start by presenting, in a short, concise manner, a summary of what SPECIFICALLY you're looking for from the sharks. Follow with the financial details and facts about the property. Remember, 4-6 minutes.
* Know what you want: ask up front (private money, interest rates, partnership, work and split, wholesale, etc.). Be specific.
* Know your numbers - Be able to discuss with confidence and ease:
    * ARV (after repair value). What is rent or sale, after repair?
    * Purchase (contract) price: Why? History? Timing on contract.
    * Details: Security? Closing costs? Your money input, if any.
* Come prepared and be thorough: knowing your numbers will catch a Shark. Unprepared, with no answers, will be Shark Bait!

Additional Tips:

* Know what you're asking for and why. Know what you will or will not accept prior to presentation.
* Shark Tank Style example: I'm looking for $80k on a home that sells for $140k, after $30k rehab, split profits, etc.
* Understand your exit strategies, marketing, and realtor. What backup, if no sale?

THE MORE KNOWLEDGEABLE YOU ARE ABOUT WHAT YOU'RE ASKING, THE BETTER YOUR CHANCES.

There is no guarantee that any of the sharks will take your deal, regardless of how *good* the deal is. It's solely up to you to convince and *sell* the Sharks on taking your deal.

Showtime

Now it's showtime, and a win-win for the investors in the audience, the investors asking for funds, and the lenders on stage. The rules are set up to give the investor guidelines to create that portfolio in such a way as to create a successful relationship with a series of lenders. Plus, rules help presenters get their info in early enough so I can put it up on display overhead. This makes it possible for the audience investors to participate and enjoy also.

Each lender publicly takes a minute to explain what type of lending they do, and what their perfect deal is. After each deal presentation, each gets another minute to declare whether they are in or out—deal or no deal. Then they explain why that deal would or would not fit their type of lending, educating the investors and the audience on what would make it a good deal for that lender.

Just in case, the Sharks are given clipboards showing how things will flow, along with some of the most common questions, and so that they can keep score.

Ready for fun?

- The stage is set with high stools so the sharks can be seen by the whole audience.
- A few sharks are hanging around the room.
- The overhead pictures are ready for intros and deals.
- Of course, there are lots of actual shark pictures in between each deal.

- Shark snacks are tossed to the audience.
- The shark music is ready

The biggest panic before showtime is having *no shark bait* appear. That's right! Can you believe it? No investors wanting money. Well, of course, all investors want money. But very few want to ask for it in public, in front of all their peers. Or they don't want to disclose their big deal. Or at least they don't want to be the first onstage.

It is easy to get the lenders to front and center—it is good advertising. Of course, the audience will show, because this is great entertainment, just listening to deals. But add the entertainment of *deal or no deal*, and it is a full house. All these parts can be set up ahead of time.

If one of the sharks don't show, you still have several others. If the audience is a little light, set up less chairs. But if no bait, there is no show.

There's a safety net for that also. As a board member duty, they get volunteered. The program for that month is to teach the audience, the investor, and the lenders. So, I beg the board investors to put a portfolio together on their latest deal, as a back-up.

It turns out that when they did do a presentation, they did well with funding their deals also.

As a matter of fact, almost every shark bait presentation got funded one way or another. This happens consistently every shark tank year.

Since it is one of our better attended events, it has become a staple in our calendar every year, right along with our annual spring Trade Fair.

Shark Bait Showcase

Shark Tank, real estate style, doesn't just stop after the last shark bait presentation.

After the presentations, every single one of the shark bait presenters gets a table to display their deals. Presenters then have an open forum to discuss their deals with any investor that may be interested. They just went through the Sharks; now they can answer just about any questions about their deals. The investors in the audience can now come join the presenters at their tables, and investigate whether the deal would work for them or not.

Remember, many investors in the audience have money sitting dormant, waiting to multiply. In this day and time, most are lucky to get one-fourth of one present on their CDs, or savings or self-directed IRAs.

Almost all of our shark tank deals have been either funded or tweaked, or were successful in ways they didn't even think about before they shared their presentation.

Part of the deal for being brave enough to be a shark bait presenter–the shark tank deals that got away–were published in our newsletter for all investors to check out.

Education-wise, the investors have learned how to put a presentation portfolio together that will wow most lenders. Investors have also learned to tweak their deals to appeal to many different types of lenders.

The local lenders have learned how to get their message out, and tweak their lending to the local market, along with having been introduced to a pool of now savvy investors.

The investor audience has learned about some new deals that are being worked on. They also viewed many different ways of presenting those deals. Also great, is the variety of lenders in our own group, ready to fund dollars if the deal is presented in a way that fits their programs.

Publish the Ones that Didn't Get Away

There's always a follow-up on Shark Tank deals from the meeting night. The editor of our *Investor's Survival Journal* does a follow-up article to appear the following month.

I have written several interviews, with pictures, but most of the deals were taken care of one way or another. They were no longer available.

So, out of necessity, we had to start doing write-ups on some of the great deals that did NOT get away.

On the programmer's side, though, I find that once a *Shark Bait* investor hooks up with a lender *Shark,* they are satisfied. They are so satisfied, they end up doing more deals with that very same lender, over and over again.

This means, at the following year's Shark Tank meeting, the programmer has to start all over again, convincing new Shark Bait to try for the pot of gold.

I actually went just outside Detroit, Michigan to view a live Shark Tank meeting, before I tried it at a local meeting. Their Shark Tank meeting was quite a bit different. It started out doing deals at small round tables. Without mics, it was a bit hard to hear what type of real estate deal each table was covering.

Then there was a stage presentation, similar to what we decided to do locally, and is covered here.

Just like real estate investing, there are a ton of different ways to put on a show. Actually, it will probably change a little every time you put one on. It will morph as your group of investors do.

We have a lot of fun with this program, and I hope you try it too.

No one said education has to be BORING.

Chapter 8

Build Your Team/Vendor Benefits

Trade Fair Shoestring

I've had a Trade Fair every year in a row for thirty years, just as spring has sprung. We started having a Trade Fair almost as soon as we added vendor and business partners. It truly is your *team-building* meeting for the rest of the year.

First, let me say that we do a trade fair on a shoestring. It is supposed to add to your finances, not run them dry; or have you working under the strain of worrying if it will break the bank if no one shows up.

We do not rent the huge hall or auditorium. The whole purpose is to give a feel of crowds and excitement for a positive response from attendee and the businesses behind the tables. I've gone to many trade fairs in convention centers, where you can hear your voice echo, and it looks like the only people attending are the vendors going from booth to booth themselves.

For the investor or the business partner, it's all about creating the energy and the feeling that the business partners can solve your investor problems, in a fun, full, carnival-like atmosphere.

It is also important that the investors can meet and remember all our business partners and their discounts at one time. In our area, spring is when everyone can get out of the house; and starting to do rehab is perfect timing for both the investor and the business partner. If you would like to try this event, I will put it in the full blueprint, on www.EnergizeSolve

Prosper. It shows how you can put 48 to 50 vendors in one hall, and create a successful event.

There is a complete setup system to completely decorate and have the Trade Fair hall completely ready in 1-2 hours. Some aspects of the setup are crucial to crowd flow, keeping the people in the Trade Fair energized; not to mention keeping the business partners engaged with the investors.

There are also some inexpensive bonuses on every vendor's table, along with a mini pizza-fueled vendor meeting, to help all tables to participate and be successful. Found at any local dollar store, for one dollar or less per item, per table, you can get bottled water, framed membership certificates, mints, helium balloons, table clothes, table skirting, and baskets for collecting cards.

4 Corner Posts

A lot of study has gone into the placement of different vendors—actually, a lot of trial and error as well. Placing vendors, with similar products, at opposite ends of the room for civility in competition, takes a blueprint and lots of brainstorming. Even if the vendors in the same profession are the best of friends, both will need some space to let the clients attending know about their product and services.

The most important idea is to have the energy in the room high and fun. If there needs to be excitement in the room, then each corner should have a special event that will keep investors constantly circling throughout the night.

I learned this concept when we used to take up three adjoining halls, and there were complaints from the third hall. No one wanted their table assigned to Hall #3 because a lot of attendees never even made it back that far. I had to create something, so we ran fifteen or thirty-minute training sessions, in the third hall only. The tables in Hall #3 were all the vendors that wanted to do mini training sessions.

That eye-opening concept led to the four-corner post rule. Creating fun spots keeps the investors and attendees constantly moving around too.

Great corner activity suggestions:

- prize boards display on the wall
- hospitality table filled with finger food, sponsored by the Toledo NW Ohio Food Bank
- vendor with a casino table cloth, giving out candy bars to winners
- vendors with popcorn machines
- auto vendors that are willing to put lease cars and truck deals out your front door
- chiropractor with vibrating chair samples
- Home Depot, with tons of giveaways
- real estate investor Info table, with one-year free membership as a giveaway
- Gutter Monkey Co, with a monkey in coveralls on a ladder, tossing candy
- vendor with presentation on a TV they will be giving away

The first three are at every one of our annual Trade Fairs.

All these fun spots will keep attendees moving around the room, and will keep the vendor tables happy.

Showtime

Your room is all set up on a shoestring but looks professional and festive. Now, all vendors have a complete setup, even if they are small and have nothing to bring but a flyer.

All your vendor members have received their vendor membership marketing packages, as soon as they sign up. Then, the weekend prior to the Trade Fair, they get a CallFire reminder message from the president, about the meeting, times for set-up, and the fifty-dollar prize all vendors bring for the prize board.

At the Trade Fair, they are getting a Trade Fair packet with an instant agenda for the evening. The Trade Fair packet also has all the marketing benefits of their membership level listed, and all the extra sponsorships that they have at their fingertips. The packet ends with a survey for that night, which must be turned in before any vendor can leave for the night.

Their table/booth is set, skirted, and covered. All vendors also have a personalized table sign, with their name. Their table also has bottles of water, Tic Tacs, and a framed certificate of their membership.

Once the vendors arrive during setup time, and the doors are almost ready to open, we have a five-minute training session, with pizza. I hand out the schedule for the evening, mention several things that can be done to create excitement in their own particular booth, and remind them they cannot leave till they check off the survey on the last page. So all surveys must be torn off, checked off, and turned in.

As for the board members and volunteers, they all have specific and important jobs to cover during the Trade Show to keep it running smoothly. Each board member is scheduled for approximately thirty to forty minutes at the investor table, for any questions or sign-ups for membership.

Then there's a group who fills, and then just keeps refilling, the food on the sponsored hospitality table: finger foods, snacks, punch, napkins, etc. They usually have a theme when decorating the hospitality goodies.

Next is the *prize board team*. They must collect all the prizes from each vendor, and catalogue and display them all overhead. That team will also go table to table and pick the prizes every ten minutes.

There are also greeters at the front door, handing out investor bags of goodies to all who walk through the door. They are also available to answer any location questions. One of their biggest jobs is to count every person that walks through that front door.

The *vendor chair* is making sure that all vendors have everything they want, with no problems. The vendors are usually trapped at their tables, so the vendor chair will grab some snacks for them, or more water, etc.

Create the Crowd

What is a Trade Fair without attendees? And why would your vendors ever come again if there wasn't a good turnout?

Let me cover a few things we do to make sure we have a lot of attendees through the door. To start with, we do it after business hours–for the most part, 7pm. We also have it on a weekday–our regular meeting night–where we always have close to 100+ investors.

Every vendor member gets signs to put in their office, or takes them to pass out.

It is the only time we are also open to the public.

All media is used, including social meetup and website meetup.

Radio ad packages have been used.

It is added to all free public calendars.

Ads are put in all neighborhood or suburb newspapers.

Our own flyers and postcards are copied and mailed or handed out.

We run ads, such as "FREE, and Open to the Public."

.....everything you ever wanted or needed for real estate investing.

- Have you ever thought of OWNING REAL ESTATE?
- Do you BUY STUFF?
- Do you like to SAVE MONEY?
- Do you like to HAVE FUN?

If the answer is YES to even 1 of these questions, then you can't afford to miss this!

Any adult attendee is eligible to WIN... and **there is no limit to the prizes you win!**

BUT...*you must be present to win.*

There are prizes every 5 minutes!

That is a big one! Advertising that there will be prizes given away every 5 minutes, and that all you have to do to win is be present, is a crowd pleaser.

There are handouts for four months, starting the first of the year. Change cabin fever to spring fever, at our Trade Fair.

We also eblast to our 4000+ investor list, using CallFire, or TextFire, and we send to all real estate offices, and use the auditors rental list.

I am sure you can think of many more in your local area. I usually get 200+ through the doors within the first twenty minutes.

Announce the Count

One of the important tasks we do is have a greeter at the front door, counting attendees and handing out goodie bags, for the first thirty minutes or so. Once the door count reaches over a couple of hundred, his job is to go to every single vendor table and let them know the exciting news.

Yes, excitedly inform him that we have already reached a couple hundred-plus attendees in the first thirty minutes. Attendance numbers mean nothing if your business partners do not know it on the spot and get excited about it too.

Our Trade Fair then becomes so energized, packed, and filled with attendees that the vendors actually ask us to quit interrupting to give away the prizes at their table. They want to have more time with the investors they are talking to.

The excitement takes place when you are excited. If you don't share it, it goes nowhere. If you share it, all the vendors catch it too.

We have all the surveys to prove it. They report it excitedly.

We used to report the attendance number at our board meeting, and the surveys were not bad but sort of bland. Once we started sharing the count at the Trade Fair, the enthusiasm and satisfied vendors rose significantly.

Left to their own, a vendor doesn't know if it's good or bad attendance. But if the numbers are announced, then the problem is at his own table, and he needs to step up his game.

We actually don't keep a count after that, at least not where the vendors are concerned. Most often, it is irrelevant, because most attendees are lined up outside when you open the doors, and they rush in.

I like to keep any total number to their imaginations. Some think that means another two hundred every thirty minutes. But we do stop by tables that are a bit crowded, and mention that they are too busy and that we will catch them later.

Let me put in a little note about surveys. When you have fifty great comments and one complainer, do not change your whole setup for the one complainer, or you'll end up with the other fifty being unhappy.

Average in all the good comments with the not so good ones. Use the ones with suggestions to tweak your event. More often than not, they are not aware that what they are asking already exists, and you need more training or exposure of what is available to all members.

Survey, Survey, Survey

I mentioned the survey before. It was the final page of info given to vendors at the Trade Fair.

Equally important is that *"they are not allowed to leave till they fill out and turn in the EZ checklist survey on the last page."*

The survey is a one-page EZ survey. It is easy and quick to fill out and return. The ten questions are marked one through five, depending on your feel for the evening. There are also a few spare lines at the bottom for any extra comments for improvement.

EXAMPLE:

Dear Vendor,

Please take a few moments to complete our evaluation sheet and turn it in on Trade Fair night **before you leave,** to any board member. It is our intent to make our annual Trade Fair professional and rewarding to all our members, guests, and vendors. Your critique of our performance is valued and appreciated.

Thank you in advance for your cooperation in this matter. President

Vendor Name: ______________________________________
                   (required for our complete evaluation)

 Please rate all answers as (1) Excellent (2) Very Good (3) Good (4) Fair (5) Poor.

1) Were you notified enough in advance?
2) Did you have enough time to set up your station?
3) How well did we accommodate your pre-requested needs?
4) Was the room layout conducive to good traffic flow?
5) Did you attend a vendor training session to optimize success?
6) Does your product/services match the needs of our members?
7) Were you satisfied with the number of guest visits?
8) How would you rate your overall satisfaction?
9) What extra information would you like to have received?
10) What could you have done to add to your success?

Please use the added lines below to offer your comments and opinions as to how we might further this event. Your general commentary, as well as input, specific to your trade, is appreciated.

Of course, all board members are assigned to make sure all surveys are collected before any vendor leaves.

It is also important to note that a pleased vendor doesn't always put anything in comments, because that vendor has no complaints. If you do get a bad one, before making changes, remember the dozens and dozens that were happy with the current results.

But still, *Survey, Survey, Survey.*

Chapter 9

Earn Designation/2-Year Small Business Degree

PHP

Let's start with the derogatory name used by government and the media wishing to attack investors: the LANDLORD.

Yeah, sure they have a few horror stories about investors, just like we have regarding tenants.

Just the same, the good *housing providers* extremely outweigh the problem ones. We prefer the name, *housing provider*, and have the education to back it up. Hopefully preventing the government from licensing and regulating investors was one of our first legal challenges.

That was one of our biggest challenges years ago. It was time to educate ourselves, PHP (professional housing provider) was the solution initiated about a decade ago. The series, PHP, is similar to a two-year college course for a small business degree, strictly in real estate investing.

It was an honor to find out, decades ago, that National REIA actually chose an Ohio style model to create their PHP model. One of the reasons was that it can be produced locally in your own meetings, and not dependent on a college.

Those that used city colleges soon lost control of the teachers and their content being fine-tuned to real estate investing. The teachers may not even know the topics as they pertain to real estate investing.

Here is a sample of the topics I cover in order to graduate:

What is the PHP designation?

The PHP designation is a nationwide, education-based certification program designed to recognize the high level of knowledge and professionalism among the designation holder. It is sponsored and overseen by the National REIA

Why obtain the PHP designation?

Only persons completing the educational requirements will be permitted to hold themselves out to the public as a Professional Housing Provider. The designee will be recognized in the form of an award certificate and the right to use the designation, and should recognize that having a basic education in the topics outlined below will increase his or her ability to reach their goals in real estate investment. Further, as National REIA works to make the PHP designation more recognizable, it is hoped that the PHP holders will have an advantage in dealing with legal and governmental bodies when a "my word against his" situation occurs. It will also aid in encouraging legislators to think of educated investors as a larger group for political action. Some classes can already be taken online through the local chapter and National REIA program.

How will I obtain these hours?

These hours may be obtained through local association meetings and seminars, OR through courses taught outside of the local groups. All outside courses and seminars must meet the following requirements: they must be taught live; they must be pre-approved by the PHP committee, and they must provide a certificate of attendance acceptable to the PHP Committee.

Continuing education to maintain PHP designation

Once the PHP designation has been obtained, designees must complete 20 hours of continuing education every two years in order to maintain the designation. These hours are elective and may be used by the designee to continue his or her education as he sees fit.

Goals of REIA

The concept of creating educated investors is important in the fight to make our industry a respected one. We also believe the ability to present our members as dedicated, educated professionals will aid in the political action to which we are dedicated. While this education is already the mission of the local associations, we hope that a statewide designation will further this goal by making legislators, regulators, and the public at large recognize that we are not simply *landlords*, but informed business persons who make an ongoing contribution to communities.

The course of study will be divided into 42 clock hours of core courses, and 18 hours of elective topics, for a total of 60 hours of formal education.

Appraisal 2 hours - Including formal appraisal methods (cost, income, and replacement), Pace instruction, how to compare properties, etc.

Contract Law 3 hours - Including basic contract law; using contracts and clauses to protect yourself; developing contracts such as leases, options, purchase contracts, etc. for the real estate investment business.

Ethics 1 hour - Including enacting and actual use of national, state, local, and personal business ethics, statements, policies, and practices.

Fair housing law 2 hours - Including federal, state, and local fair housing regulations.

Finance 6 hours - Including conventional financing, FHA/VA financing, owner financing of all types; comparing financing, offering financing.

Inspections 2 hours - Including pre and post purchase inspections, and pre and post move-out inspections of properties held.

Insurance 3 hours
Property 1 hour - Including what type of property insurance is appropriate for investment property; negotiating for the best rates, and renters insurance.
Worker's compensation 1 hour - Including when, why, and for whom to carry worker's compensation insurance.
Liability 1 hour - Including why and how much

Landlord Tenant Law 2 hours - Including landlord and tenant responsibilities, evictions, etc.

Management 4 hours - Including record keeping, dealing with tenants, maximizing cash flow, and others.

Marketing 2 hours - Including how to market properties for sale and for rent; how to market buying services.

Negotiation 3 hours - Includes negotiating with sellers, buyers, renters, contractors and vendors, banks, etc.

Purchasing 2 hours - Including finding deals and calculating profitability.

Rehab 4 hours
Classroom 2 hours - Including estimation, which projects will pay for themselves, etc.
Hands-on 2 hours - Including actual hands-on opportunities and demonstrations.

Regulations 4 hours
EPA 1 hour - Including regulations affecting real estate investment, such as lead paint regulations, wetlands regulations, underground storage tank regulations, Environmental Quality Zone regulations, etc.
Federal 1 hour - Including regulations affecting real estate investment other than tax laws, fair housing laws, and EPA regulations.
Local 2 hours - Including zoning and building codes.

Tax law 2 hours
Income 1 hour - Includes calculating and minimizing tax, and tax laws as they affect real estate investors.
Other 1 hour - Including property taxes, 1031 tax deferred trades, etc.

The remaining 18 hours may include further education in any or all of the above topics, as selected by the OPHP candidate.

Meeting Driver

Another great benefit of a PHP style education is that it's a great method of driving people towards your meetings on a regular basis. It will fill the seats with those investors wanting the needed education.

Just imagine that a programmer has a year and half of needed topics to cover for all investors. The ability to create *business oriented* investors is one of the prime goals to keep government from mandating their own laws and rules for investors.

Any members that have started down the road to becoming a *professional housing provider,* or even just to get educated on real estate investing, can't pass up a free program to do so.

In general, it will take a year and a half to two years to roll through all the mandatory topics to graduate as a professional housing provider. Investor members have made that education commitment. That will keep your seats filled for almost two years, not even counting all the electives they need after that.

Not only does that give you varied and thorough educational programs, but it creates educated investors that will stay in business longer, maybe even for decades.

A lot of other cities use the PHP program as a fundraiser, with workshops and boot camps. They also have special events when their investors ask for the extra hours needed.

I really prefer to keep PHP as the basic education at every monthly meeting, which is always free for all members. At the end of each one of our meetings, you can pick up your PHP certificate right at the rear of the room. Then record them on the back page of our manual to keep track of what topic you have accomplished.

Don't get me wrong, we do have workshops, and quite a few every year. They are also certified as one of the available towards your PHP designation.

I cannot emphasize enough how wonderful an education program is for filling your rooms each and every month with investors and future investors.

Making your meetings full is one thing, but making your meetings full of investors, wanting more and more education every month, is a fantastic feeling of accomplishment.

It goes a long way towards my goal of having every one of the investors at every one of our meetings every month.

Create 2 Two Year Loyalty

Such a robust training or education schedule creates a loyal assembly of investors educated enough to run a successful business. Quite often, real estate investing is not the first choice, or the professional goal of someone just starting out.

More often than not, an investor ends up in real estate from a need to put money to work somewhere, to create a return on their money. Another reason for real estate investing is simply when a house did not sell, and now it's a rehab, or it becomes a rental accidentally.

It goes something like this. A person moves, but their house never sells, so out of self-defense, financially, the family has to rent it out. The first renters are usually the kids or relatives. Before you know it, you're renting to the grandkids, and most of the time, there is no actual rent paid. Now that you have run out of family and friends, you are renting to the general public.

Now you really are in business, without even knowing how you got there. If you're in the business, you need to know how to run a business. There are a lot of get-rich-quick schemes, and speakers that will spend your money for you when you are looking for info.

Instead, a steadier, healthier path is learning from those that are local, and doing it every day in your own area. Add to that, getting education and courses that pertain strictly to real estate investing are hard to come by.

A number of local area investors group together and use PHP to inexpensively learn the basics. It also touches on all the different avenues a person can take in real estate investing. I'm glad to offer full instruction manuals and topic descriptions. on www.AnnaMillsPro.com. In meetings like our investor groups, this is taught at every monthly meeting, with zero extra cost to members.

So, as mentioned earlier, your local investor will generally make a commitment, even if it is just in their own mind, to show up for the free meetings and education. That commitment seems to last a minimum of two or more years. They view it as a bonus education program, all ready and waiting for them every month.

More often than not, by then, they are hooked on not only the education but the fun and the great networking with other local investors that they have made friends or business links with.

Programmer's Dream

Programs for real estate investor meetings seems like a never ending task. The meetings roll by, month by month, and turn into years of meetings, which all need a valid but interesting educational topic. Quite often, you find yourself choosing the same topic over and over again, only to realize that you just covered that topic a few months back.

Getting updated, fresh topics that are adding to the education needed seems like a brain twister after a few years in business. I have run a local REIA for more than thirty years, so my brain is twisted most of the time.

Whenever I heard new material as a realtor, or even as a contractor, I would jump on it as a possible meeting for investors. Usually, when I delve deeper, it really is not for the investor at all. Even if it can be tweaked to serve the needs of investors, there is much more work to do. Trying to find a qualified speaker on the subjects is one thing. Finding a speaker that you can try to change their whole outlook on is entirely more difficult.

When PHP showed up giving an outline of 21 separate possible topics, it was unbelievable. The stress relief was almost immediate. To have each topic certified was the cream on top.

Following such needed topics as PHP has to offer is a programmer's dream. A group of investors can cover all the major education needs in their general meetings alone. This robust program allows a different but important topic to be covered throughout a year and a half, without repeating.

It is like taking a two-year business course, strictly in real estate investing! There was even a protocol for getting local businesses to become certified to teach investors.

There are some pretty easy rules to get local talent certified in the needed topics. In preparing for investor education sessions, your editor normally needs all your advertising info early, and needs to gather the needed stuff, such as picture, bio, outline, or bullet points for the front page, and some pertinent articles to print. Having someone in charge go through the information, and usually the outline, sets up for great and pertinent education. This creates a great newsletter, a great speaker, and a great class.

Let's use contracts for an example topic. After the basics are checked out, their outline may need to be strictly real estate investor related. If, amongst their bullet points, I am finding it to be all owner occupied, a change is needed.

I would request they change it to concentrate on multiple offers, and presenting low offers, or dual offers, etc. It becomes a win-win solution because the investors are getting what they need, and the agent is a more relevant educator. A bonus for the presenter is that they are now certified as an investor in that topic, and can speak in other investor groups.

Graduation

Education, to your assembly of investors, will be as important to them as it is to any of the leaders. Investors will be as excited about education as the presenters are about teaching their topic. PHP (professional housing providers) has formal rules and regulations to its curriculum, just like any other certification. Once you have achieved the correct credits and electives, you have completed the series.

This includes a graduation every year, on a National level, at their midyear training event.

Trying to get to graduation is a priority for some of the

investors. They often are checking how many credits they have, and how many they still need. I also get a lot of requests to repeat certain topics, because they missed it and still want to keep working towards completion and graduation.

The PHP credit for the meeting that night is announced at the beginning of every meeting. Everyone in attendance is pointed towards the PHP manual, in the back, with the certificates they will pick up at the end of the meetings.

Tracking your credits is also different with each city. Locally, we issue certificates and a manual to go with them. The manual also lists all the mandatory topics needed to graduate. The official manual answers any frequently asked questions about getting to graduation, such as:

How will I obtain these hours?

These hours may be obtained through local association meetings and seminars, OR through courses taught outside of the local groups. All outside courses and seminars must meet the following requirements: they must be taught live; they must be pre-approved by the PHP committee, and they must provide a certificate of attendance acceptable to the PHP Committee.

Goals

National Real Estate Investor's Association is dedicated to making this program a success. It is understood by the committee that the program will evolve as time goes on, and that time will pass before the local groups, their members, and the public at large, recognizing the value of this education. National REIA believes the concept of creating educated investors is important in the fight to make our industry a respected one. We also believe the ability to present our members as dedicated, educated professionals will aid in the political action to which we are dedicated. While this education is already the mission of the local associations, we hope that a statewide designation will further this goal by making legislators, regulators, and the public at large recognize that we are not simply *landlords*, but informed business persons who make an ongoing contribution to communities.

The local tracking of credits is done on the back of the four-page manual. There is a simple graph that you can add each certificate to. When there are topics missing, I can schedule a mini workshop to cover what is needed to graduate. Once the requirements are filled, you graduate at the National REIA event, with grads all around the nation.

Once a graduate, you are still not left alone to fend for your own education. Once the PHP designation has been obtained, designees must complete 20 hours of continuing education, every two years, in order to maintain the designation. These hours are elective and may be used by the designee to continue his or her education as he sees fit.

Monthly Recognition

Recognition of those who have attained the next level, through graduation, is vital. It is a wonderful and professional designation they have worked for and attained.

I mentioned that grads are honored at the graduation nationally, but that is just the first step. There is also a local graduation in front of their peers upon return, which is just as important. This acclamation is repeated again at the Holiday Meeting, at the end of the year, when we also recognize all our volunteers.

We don't stop there. All graduates, from throughout the years, are recognized at the start of every new year, and are asked to stand. I want the audience to see how many people around them are serious investors. I want everyone there to know which investors are educated. I want all investors to know who to direct their tough questions to.

It's a big deal, and you need to make it a big deal by putting your graduate's accomplishments before the whole group as much as possible. I like to do it at the beginning of every meeting, when we ask if there are any buyers, sellers, etc. I also ask how many new graduates and how many previous PHP grads are in the audience.

I want to show how proud I am of all the investors that took time to take their knowledge to the next level. This, in turn, will show the rest of the attendees what to strive for. Graduates are now business savvy. They are the ones we ask to help us as volunteers. Well, we are all volunteers, but choosing a graduate means you have someone who can accomplish something. A graduate is someone you can plan on sticking with it to the end. A graduate is someone who can answer questions correctly at your meetings.

Chapter 10

International Investing Education Vacation

Secret of International Travel

International real estate investing is a wonderful *education vacation.* I first learned the concept when my vice president worked in Mexico City. He was traveling throughout Latin countries every year, for extremely reasonable prices. I wanted to know how that worked.

The first question I just had to ask was how this could be so affordable—Puerto Vallarta, Cabo San Lucas, Dominican, Costa Rica, Playa del Carmen, Mexican Riviera, Yucatan Peninsula, the pyramids, Acapulco, Belize, and many more locations.

This local Latin history was the secret to his inexpensive travel successes. I learned that Latin families all over the world pilgrimage to their local *all-inclusive* packages, for a fortnight every Christmas holiday season, December through January. This has been a Latin custom for generations.

Being the investor mind that we all are, he checked into the prices. He checked for the best prices and found out that the week before their holyday pilgrimage, the all-inclusive hotels are decorated to the hilt for the holidays, but are almost empty.

The price reduction packages during this pre-season time are amazingly affordable. All-inclusive does mean the airfare, and all the food and drink, in a five-star resort hotel on the water. Sounds pretty good for investors who are known to be very careful with their spending.

This is how our thirty-year international travel tradition started. Not to mention that this time of the year can easily be a level three, closed streets kind of freezing.

There are a few conditions you have to be ready for. When the sale price is announced, usually sometime around August or September, everyone has to be ready to jump on it. The sale price might only be available for 72 hours or maybe a little more. The package may be available a little longer than that, but the price may raise as the plane fills up. So, readiness is the key up front.

For planning purposes, the investors always know, every year, that it is going to fall in the first or second week of December. It is almost always from weekend to weekend. It always starts at the best price, and rises. So, it is first come, first served; with the best prices.

You need to have all your documents in order. Today, that is pretty normal for travel anytime, anywhere. You will be traveling with a group, but it even includes your airfare.

Most often, a deposit is all that is needed up front to secure the great price.

Most prices have been good enough to bring my daughter from California to partner up with my mom— they enjoy these international planning sessions.

Investor Family

When our local investors get together, we prefer to allow doubles memberships.

I encourage doubling with a business partner, a family member, or another investor. It always helps to have encouragement and assistance from a partner or family member on real estate projects. It also is a great help when the family gets a better idea of what it is that you do for a living.

Family involvement brings education and understanding all the way around to full circle. I try to schedule several family/partner style events throughout the year. A few of the family friendliest are the December international planning sessions, the Trade Fair open to the public, the year-end Holiday Extravaganza, and the National REIA educational cruise every winter.

I mentioned earlier that the international planning session, each year in December, is a family-oriented excursion. Since it is partner and family oriented, I bring my daughter from the west coast to partner up with my ninety-year-old mom.

As a matter of fact, I have to write permission slips to get my ninety-year-old mother out of her two college classes to join us every year. She has always been an entrepreneur at heart. Mom always wants to do something new that she has never done before each year. I am amazed, as she has tried zip lining and parasailing in the last few years.

As we set up the agenda for each day, it is really nice to get family comments, whether they are involved in real estate or not.

Annual Planning Session

As it turns out, for the price of a stuffy hotel room and food for our annual planning meeting, vs. the international all-inclusive, they were quite comparable and much more family oriented.

There is a lot more attendance when it is international and family oriented rather than being locked up with local winter weather to do the next year's planning.

In my region, that time of the year is often met with level 3 snow and closed roads. The planning session for the following year works quite well under a palm tree, and with family input.

Our planning sessions are held following the free breakfast everyone just finished. Everyone must be signed in on the attendance sheet if they want a copy for their records or for their tax preparer. That is about as formal as we get.

I already have a list of the five or six problem areas we want to correct. Sometimes it will also be something new we want to try in the upcoming year.

Often, different topics and events we learned about at National REIA, midyear, will be some of the topics also. Are they something that will fit into our local real estate investing? If it looks promising, how would we add it to our schedule or agenda?

Family might not always understand the full details of what we are discussing, but they throw in any thoughts they may have. Talk about thinking outside the box. It is amazing what a non-investor comment can start.

We tackle a different problem or topic each day. It is then given out with the papers, to jot down any other comments during the day. It can be while you are on excursions, or just lying in the sun (not the snow).

With plenty of brainstorming throughout the day, the comments, by the end of the day, are quite imaginative and plentiful. Most sessions are wrapped up around dinnertime, which seems to be close to eight o'clock in foreign countries.

The wrap-up usually takes place at the free dinner buffet, or at specialty restaurants included in the package.

Investor members can keep their own packets or turn them in at the end of the day, to be passed out the next morning. The organizer is in charge of the possession of all documents and sign-in sheets.

Some of the general improvement topics are pretty similar to the following:

WHAT MAKES A GOOD REIA?
- Successful members
- Leadership
- Education
- Experienced members give back
- Giving value/benefits
- Balance

- Market/stats
- Core group of passionate leaders
- Operations perfected
- Ethics
- Strategic planning every year
- Business partners
- Financial stability

COMPLAINTS
- Other REIAs or expensive boot camps
- Taken advantage of
- Lack of leadership
- Poor meetings
- Pitched pyramid schemes
- Lack of focus/ boring
- Landlord vs. entrepreneurial

PUBLIC
- Get on the front page for NWO Foodbank
- Local city council contacts
- Dress code for board members

WHAT ARE MEMBERS PAYING FOR?
- Education
- Networking
- Stats
- Guidance
- Mentoring
- Results
- Learning how to make money

WHAT WOULD YOUR MEMBER MISS THE MOST (IF CUT)?
- Recognition at end of year
- Mandatory orientation
- Networking

- Leaders leaving
- Sense of community
- Market update

Once the results are compiled and typed up, a copy is sent to all that had signed in. The full report, with all suggestions, is taken to the next board meeting. If there was a quorum in attendance at the international planning session, different parts may already be voted in.

Viewing Local RE Customs

At the Annual International Planning session, days are filled up with family adventures, meeting with local realtors and business owners, as well as the local sites.

It turns out, even decades ago, local international real estate offices had the tools to do international contracts on the internet, with multiple language printouts, long before the U.S. Even today, local real estate offices do not have the routine ability to print out sales contracts in multiple languages, at the touch of a button.

It was so easy to fill out the offers we wished to make, and have it immediately so everyone could read them in their own language. There was so much clarity, especially when you were making changes and counters back and forth.

It was not so modern in regard to having local transportation to see the properties. There was usually only one real estate office-shared vehicle. So, property showings were a waiting game for the return of the sole vehicle.

But we always worked it out and had fun doing it. There's nothing like stuffing a whole group of investors into a Volkswagen, the local taxi vehicle. Days spent viewing land or properties, learning the local customs, and learning to buy in different countries was exhilarating.

The biggest bonus, of course, was the money exchange

profit. I almost always had a minimum of 10 to 1 of our dollars. The prices were really reasonable once you figured in the exchange rate for that day. I probably put many offers on villas, and dozens of rentals.

Investors that love looking at properties anyhow are in their glory while the snow falls back home.

Due diligence is imperative for making offers. In other words, that means checking out and learning the local customs on real estate—the local customs on buying and selling, not to mention taxes, etc.

The last thing you want to do is insult a buyer or seller, or government official, without even knowing it, because their customs are far different than ours.

Disrespecting someone is the best way to all of a sudden have no one speak English, and you are on your own.

Bartering is a lesson needed in almost all countries I have visited. The locals are almost insulted if you do not haggle with them about the price.

Making Foreign Offers

My first year that I actually broke down and joined the international group, we visited Acapulco on the Bay. I never missed an international trip after that date. It is addictive, but it is also hard to explain how power packed and invigorating it is. It is so much more than you ever imagined it could be.

Also, on my first visit, we visited the Century 21 office, right across the street from our all-inclusive. Being with Century 21 for thirty-seven years, I was sure this would be a great adventure.

This was the real estate office that was tech savvy but vehicle poor. When the office vehicle did show up, we hit the road, and we noticed the differences right away. Everything was stone and concrete structures, usually with beautiful tile work throughout—amazing. We mentioned the fact to our local real estate agent, and it was his turn to be amazed.

He just could not fathom the concept that anyone would build a structure out of wood. After all, wood is a fuel, not a building material.

Another major difference was that none of the commercial, and only some of the residential, buildings were finished. They all had a second or third story that was basically just rebar sticking up in the air. The realtor's explanation reminded us of some techniques back home. The reason the buildings all looked half-finished was because, as soon as you finished your building, it would be taxed.

I guess a tax loophole is a loophole in any country.

We put a nice contract together with a group of investors and our attending investors on site, with an Acapulco notary. One of the biggest bonuses, which I mentioned before, is that most foreign countries' exchange rates were running at least ten to one.

This means our American dollars were worth ten times their value in most Latin countries. Some countries and islands are republics, or attached to the US, making offers easier than you would think. Other countries were very laid back, and we waited weeks and weeks for any answers to our offers.

No hurry there.

Buying real estate is different in every country, including local. In a lot of places, it is not something a person is able to do for their family.

Buying as a foreigner is actually forbidden and against the law in some places. Outsiders cannot own property on their own.

Some countries sell real estate through banks, and not through real estate companies. In some countries, you have to have a local notary do all the offers. A notary there, is similar to an attorney here.

Worldwide Flavor

There's a lot to be said about the worldwide flavor and fresh aspects of international real estate investing. The different laws alone are staggering at times. In Mexico, we had to register with a bank notary, similar to our attorneys. In some places, it is not the norm for people to own their own homes or land.

In other countries, they do allow outside or foreign ownership, but there are many more hoops to jump through because you are a foreigner. Then other countries think nothing of taking weeks and months to move along on an offer to purchase.

In some countries, the government can change their minds and the rules at will. So, quite often, you are on your own. You can be an owner one day, and it is gone to the government the next day of the government changes.

This is all part of the challenge and mystique of each new adventure. We did note that you can buy time shares just about anywhere.

Planning house, building, or resort showings for a day is quite educational. But it is more of an adventure. It is often more interesting than the excursion you can purchase from the all-inclusives.

Education can be anything you want to learn in real estate investing.

After forty-plus years, I'm still learning something every time I get together with other investors. The greatest education is right in the room, sitting next to you.

So don't be afraid to speak up and ask questions. Ask out loud to a group of investors, and get lots of answers.

I often listen and hear how someone took care of a problem, and it was *so* ingenious—something with a twist. I guarantee you, I will be doing it that way tomorrow.

ABOUT THE AUTHOR

President of Toledo
Real Estate Investors Association

Anna Mills, elected 2017 president of National REIA, continues bringing even more benefits for our local chapters. Anna was chosen because she has taken Toledo REIA to the top in Ohio and National for many years. She is also past president of Ohio Real Estate Investors (OREIA), and is currently serving as local president of Toledo REIA. Toledo Real Estate Investors Assn is a nonprofit, educational association that educates investors and entrepreneurs to earn Ohio and National Professional Housing Provider status.

Anna has been a realtor in Ohio and Michigan for 40+ years. Anna holds top designations in VIP Relocation, Investor Specialist, Property Tax Reduction, and Court Appraisals. She has received the Ruby Award, more than once, for a great mix of educating buyers, sellers, and investors on getting results.

Early in her career, she became a builder and an investor, and started acquiring properties (no money down). She currently holds 14 professional real estate and contactors licenses, including the skills trades of plumbing, heating, electrical contractor, lead paint supervisor and contractor, and Clearance Tech for lead paint.

Besides rebuilding Toledo neighborhoods, one rehab house at a time, Toledo REIA also created the Donate-a-House program, with all the profits going back into the community, through Northwest Ohio Food Bank.

As co-author of the *Landlord/Tenant Handbook*, she also speaks at, and teaches, investor workshops for the local housing authority, nationwide REIAs, and area banks. She has spoken as far away as Australia and New Zealand, through Lourdes College. Anna is past president of Toastmasters, with an Advanced Toastmaster (CTM) Silver designation; and she has been a member of Women's Council of Realtors (WCR), and Women's Entrepreneurial Network (WEN).

Anna has appeared, for several years, in *Who's Who of American Women*. She is featured in many real estate books, including *Millionaire Real Estate Investor*, and in a full chapter, in *Wise Women in Real Estate*. Number one bestselling author, Anna Mills, was interviewed in *Business Leader Interviews*, which debuted #1 on the Amazon 2016 bestseller list. She is also the author of the upcoming book, *Energize Solve Prosper - Insider Guide to Jumpstart Your Real Estate Investing*.